Leaders around the world are talking about *How to Build an Effective Board...*

"Having served on a total of 18 Boards of Directors...[I know] this book is an excellent tool....[It has] well thought out sections that make reading and learning a real pleasure. Richards has captured the essence of success for Boards around the world."
— *Jerre L. Stead, Past Chairman and CEO,*
AT&T Global Information Solutions

"Richards' concepts are refreshing...they're not a set of lofty academic theories but hard, practical lessons...principles to transform...from a passive role into a dynamic leadership relevant to Boards of all types. I heartily recommend this book."
— *Richard L. Thompson, Group President, Caterpillar Inc.*

"I am impressed by this book...there is a great need [for it].... Boards must reconstruct themselves in order to effectively lead progressive organizations. Richards' examples spotlighting good governance practices are particularly excellent."
— *R. William Taylor, CAE, President,*
American Society of Association Executives

"Societies and companies, facing tremendous challenges of change, require leadership principles and capabilities which go beyond current best practices. I recommend this book because it describes a quantum leap forward in board effectiveness. In my three years of experience with this model, I have experienced its power of taking visions to reality, building team spirit, achieving consensus decisions and getting all stakeholders to respond with empowerment in a constructive fashion."
— *Eberhard C. Stotko, Chairman,*
European Automotive Initiative Group

"This book addresses an area that's ripe for improvement.... Richards lays out a detailed 'soup-to-nuts' recipe for creating a successful Leadership....[*How to Build an Effective Board*] represents] a disciplined, comprehensive, and compelling approach to maximize Board effectiveness."
—*G. Richard Wagoner, Jr., President,*
North American Operations, General Motors Corporation

"I'm impressed with [Richards'] charisma and the leadership with which he helped re-engineer an almost century old organization. This book, based on those successful experiences, contains very valuable information to all management people—particularly is a 'must' for those who are involved in running a non-profit organization throughout the world."
— *Takashi Nakajima-san, Executive Director, SAE of Japan, Inc.*

"Richards' book has attracted my sincere interest. The theme is a burning topic of today....[*How to Build an Effective Board*] will be very useful for managers working in countries with emerging economies. It includes analyses, syntheses, and practical recommendations...."
— *I.P. Ksenevitch, Vice President, Russian Engineering Academy*

"As a professional speaker, I quickly recognize talented communicators. Richards simplifies complex organizational issues and masterfully works to train, explain, facilitate, and help build up leaders. [*How to Build an Effective Board*] is interspersed with flowing encouragement to leaders to 'ratchet up' beyond traditional processes of the past and create an effective culture of empowerment for tomorrow."
— *Peter Low, America's #1 Success Authority*

How to Build an Effective Board

R.R. Richards

asae

The author has worked to ensure that all information in this book is accurate as of the time of publication and consistent with standards of good practice in the general management community. As research and practive advance, however, standards may change. For this reason, it is recommended that readers evaluate the applicability of any recommendation in light of particular situations and changing standards.

Elissa M. Myers, CAE, ASAE Vice President and Publisher
Linda Munday, ASAE Director of Book Publishing

Editor and Production Manager:
Marianna Nunan, Gravel Hill Communications, Beltsville, Md.
Designer: Cindy Dyer, Dyer Design, Alexandria, Va.

American Society of Association Executives
1575 I Street, N.W.
Washington, DC 20005
(202)626-2723
Fax (202)408-9634

ISBN 0-88034-126-2

This book is available at a special discount when ordered in bulk quantities. For information, contact ASAE Member Services at (202)371-0940. A complete catalog of titles is available on the ASAE home page at http://www.asaenet.org

Table of Contents

Board Leadership, The Engineered Organizational Model, The Governance Model, Governance Model—Tool for an Effective Board, Four Policy Segments, Principles of the Governance Model, Governance Model Assumptions

Definition of an Effective Board, Characteristics of an Effective Board, Expectations for the Board, Key Job Products and Responsibilities of the Board, Other Board Responsibilities

ENDs Policies, Importance of Visioning, Visioning—An Analogy, Qualities of Visions, Vision Statement Do Nots, ENDs Versus Objectives, ENDs and Missions, Critical Issues, Strategic Plan, Key Result Areas, Mind the Goals and Actions for Progress, Examples of Vision Policies, Vision or Mission?

Governance—Board Business, Governance Process Policies, Clarify and Document Job Products of the Board, Job Products of the Board, Role of the President, Board Member Responsibilities, Governance Model Policies Serve as a Filter for Agendas, Governing Style, Timely Leadership—Before and After, Monitoring the Governance Process, The Board Does Tasks

Foreword

As I look around at the vast and diverse world of associations, I see that we are all faced with a multitude of issues that challenge us to succeed in the future. Foremost among these issues are:

- Practicing effective governance and strong leadership
- Establishing and pursuing a vision
- Recruiting and maintaining membership
- Using limited resources efficiently and effectively

What's the answer to confronting and taking control of these issues? Good governance and excellence in leadership. This book presents a useful model that will help you lead your association and successfully address the changes and challenges of the future.

How to Build an Effective Board teaches association executives and volunteer leaders how to empower themselves and association staff—thus empowering the association itself. The two models presented by Richards make complex concepts easy to understand; readers will be able to readily apply his concepts and strategies to their own situations. Readers also will find the appendices a treasure trove of practical and usable tools to get them started in the right direction.

How to Build an Effective Board lights the way to a shining future for you and your association.

R. William Taylor
President
American Society of Association Executives

Preface

Be prepared to be different! Abraham Lincoln said, "A mind stretched by a new idea never returns to its original dimension." This book contains a wealth of ideas that are at the cutting edge of organizational development for the future. Prepare to be different!

Change is coming. In our contemporary environment embracing movement from the industrial age to the information age, transforming leadership is more vital than ever. Organizations need a good model integrating policy, people, and provisions for success in the future. Read on!

Chapter 1

Two Models for Building an Effective Board

Board Leadership

Your organization exists to make a difference—to make contributions to society through the combined efforts of all the people of your organization. How can an organization make the most gains? How can an organization achieve the greatest results? It begins with the board of directors. The board of directors must rise to the challenge of providing overall leadership to help the organization be effective, proficient, and focused in its efforts.

Boards frequently find themselves spending time on trivial issues; thinking short term and inwardly; taking a reactive stance; and reviewing lengthy, detailed reports. Board governance often is misunderstood, undeveloped, and ill-defined. Boards often get bogged down in detailed issues and struggle with the "rubber stamp syndrome" because there seems to be too much to do. Agendas get crammed with too many items and issues, and board members become dissatisfied and frustrated.

To help move beyond the problems at hand, leaders need to be open to new opportunities and styles of thinking. Boards that rely solely on past history are on a death spiral. World-class organizations of the future will have to go through the process of finding good governance for themselves. Good leaders always are seeking new systems, methods, and techniques to reengineer and continuously improve the efficiency and effectiveness of their organization. An effective tool that can offer leveraged improvements in governance is the engineered organizational model.

The Engineered Organizational Model

The engineered organizational model may be visualized as a machine labeled "cogs of the organization." This overall organizational model may be used to define and establish the fundamental relationships for leadership understanding. This model depicts and represents the major components for a successful organization and visually describes and demonstrates how these pieces fit together for success.

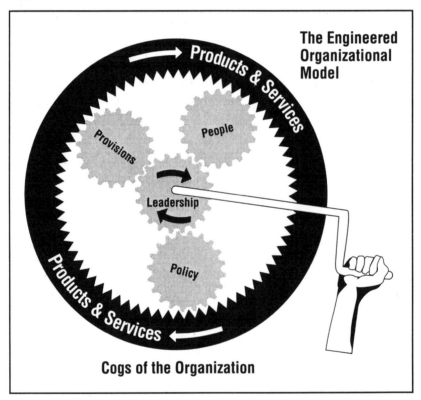

Cogs of the Organization

Leadership is fundamental to the success of any organization. As exhibited in the model, leadership can be used to leverage and activate the three cogs of policy, people, and provisions into a powerful machine for creating products and services for customers. Leadership is the beginning. It is a prerequisite and a driver of all three cogs. Leadership is fundamental.

The first cog is **policy.** This includes the governance model. It can be used to make a significant difference and markedly increase effectiveness of the organization. This model is a tool to help describe vision and direction, simplify the decision-making and communication process, and interpret *how we want to work together.*

The next cog is **people.** People are what make things happen. It is people who are most important for success. This element focuses the experience, capability, and leadership of all the special individuals who contribute to organizational success. In addition, member and staff relationships, training, teamwork, and consensus thinking make up this component to describe *who must work together.*

The third cog is **provisions.** This is the cog of the organization that could be referred to as the financial resources. Stable fiscal practices can contribute significantly to organizational success. The corporate treasures are *what must work together* to make progress for the future.

Each of these cogs of policy, people, and provisions should be strong. If one of these cogs is weak or is missing, then the capability of the organization is lessened and the amount of products and services will be less than the potential. It takes the strength and balance of all three of these component cogs to leverage leadership and optimize the products and services of the organization. With good leadership and strong policy, people, and provisions, the organization can affect powerfully the membership and their customers.

The Governance Model

The governance model is the policy cog of the engineered organizational model. For a board of directors to be effective and successful, all board members must be functioning with a common basis to advance the purposes of the organization. This governance model is a significant tool for leveraging leadership to cause optimum advancement of the organization.

Governance Model—Tool for an Effective Board

A good tool of governance is indispensable for an effective board. In today's fast-moving and sometimes hectic business environment, even good leaders will miss key opportunities for positive growth, especially if they do not have a good system of governance. Too often, progress will be slower than desired or expected. Ironically, because of the modern environment of rapid change, more opportunities exist than ever before for those with the systems thinking to harvest the rewards. According to Peter M. Senge, "systems thinking is the fifth discipline because it is the conceptual cornerstone...knowledge and tools make patterns clearer and help us see how to change them effectively...systems thinking is needed more than ever because we are becoming overwhelmed by complexity...." Systems thinking is critical, and tools, such as the governance model, are increasingly important.

Governance systems thinking is the conscious desire and capability to create and implement tools for accelerating the advancement of the organization's purpose. Systems thinking as applied to the governance of an organization can yield great gains.

Although there is no magic wand that will solve all the problems of an organization, good governance systems thinking is a key to building and achieving effective boards for successful organizations of the future. That key to success involves leveraging leadership and using proficient tools (such as the governance policy model) along with proactive teams (the people who must work together) and productive financial treasures (all the budgetary resources for day-to-day operations as well as foundation and other funds growth) of the organization.

Tools for governance should involve a practical, workable governance system that can be learned quickly, personalized effectively, and applied powerfully to produce outstanding results for the organization. This governance model helps to guide leadership with a global view for the future to meet the changes, challenges, and opportunities that lie ahead.

Four Policy Segments

In *Boards That Make a Difference,* John Carver describes four policy categories that are important for board involvement: ENDs, governance process, relationships, and limitations. According to Carver, boards should work consciously to develop policies in only these four areas. Developing a policy that does not fit one of these four policy segments, by definition, is not board work.

The four policy segments can be used to visualize a governance policy model or governance model, which is the policy cog of the engineered organizational model. These four segments are the basis for forming a policy manual for the board of directors. The policy manual should contain sections for policies in the following categories:

- **ENDs Policies**—These policies contain statements of vision and long-range direction for the organization. They answer any portion or all of the questions: what good, for whom, at what cost. Usually they occur in sets subordinate to a vision statement and define detail of the vision.
- **Governance Process Policies**—These policies document the philosophy of governance used by the board. They define how the organization is governed. They also may define officer position descriptions and board job products.
- **Relationships Policies**—These policies describe the passing of power throughout the organization. They identify delegation of authority and clarify roles, expectations, job products, and monitoring for subordinate groups and staff.
- **Limitations Policies**—These policies, written in negative language, define the limits and boundaries of acceptable means-related activity within which subordinate groups and staff must operate. All processes, operations, methods, and activities must perform within these parameters.

The policy manual serves as the primary leadership tool for the organization. It also serves as a filter to sift out board-level issues and is used to help create proactive board agendas. Non-board decisions are left to other groups within the organization.

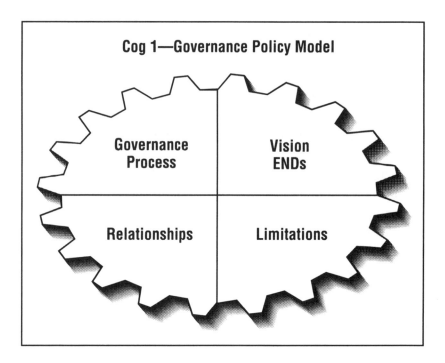

Sound policy promotes, supports, and propels empowerment.

Empowered organizations have outcomes that are results-oriented, outward-looking, fast-acting, and superior in performance over nonempowered ones that are means-driven, inward-looking, and sluggish.

The governance model provides policy for empowerment by answering fundamental leadership issues of vision, values, authority, and roles. The board's vision and direction are expressed in the ENDs policies. The board's shared expressions of values are documented in the governance process, relationship, and limitations policies:

- The board's role is clarified through the governance process policies.
- The subordinate group and staff roles and expectations are defined in the relationships policies.
- The boundaries of acceptable actions of subordinate groups and staff are shown in the limitations policies.

Applying the governance model can improve the efficiency of board meetings. Instead of being faced with a barrage of subjects, the board will spend focused time on opportunities and dreams for the future.

Principles of the Governance Model

Understanding the governance model is made easier by understanding its two major principles. First, board policies should be separated into the two major categories of *whats* and *hows*. This translates into ENDs and means. Second, board policies should be layered for direction and control.

Policies Should Be Separated into ENDs and Means

The two categories of *whats* (ENDs) and *hows* (means) describe the two broadest areas for categorizing board policy. The whats include vision and direction policies as expressed by the organization's ENDs statements. All other policy is, by definition, means policy. Keeping a mental differentiation of ends and means helps to identify good and well-crafted board policy. Separating policies into the two categories of ends and means will help you understand how to craft the best vision statements as independent and separate from means policies.

Develop Layered Policies

Policy statements are the collective and mutually agreed-upon expressions of the board's values at the broadest level. By dealing with broad board-level issues, these policies can help shape subordinate group and staff decisions. This principle, according to Carver, can be described as layered policies that may be visualized as nesting bowls. All board policies can be thought of as layered from the largest and most encompassing on the outside, to the smallest on the inside. The outside policy is the broadest and the inner ones are more detailed, supportive, and definitive. With this framework, the board must define the largest, broadest policy

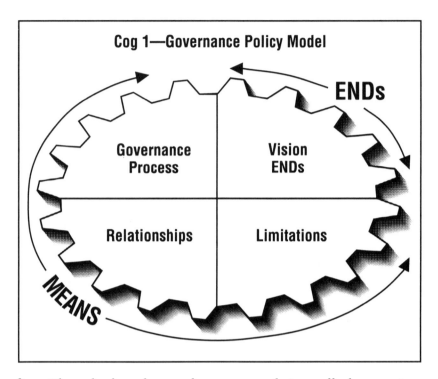

first. Then the board may choose to work inwardly by creating inner levels of detail for policy clarification.

Organizationally, subordinate groups may create their own inner policy as long as it is inside what has been defined by the board. The bowls are arranged so the board of directors' policies (the largest bowls) guide the subordinate and functional groups that report to the board. These groups then are empowered to make their own decisions and policies and to take actions as long as they're consistent with the utterances of the board. The board, therefore, leads, guides, directs, and controls the whole of the organization through a relatively small number of macro policies. By sticking with broad issues, one board was able to move from a four-foot-tall stack of past minutes, guidelines, recommendations, policies, decisions, and so forth, to a simple policy manual of fewer than fifty pages.

Effective boards must create the broad policies first, then create as many inner (detailed) policies as necessary to effectively communicate the values and vision to the organization. The board stops creating inner policies when it feels comfortable accepting any reasonable interpretation of all the policy statements. The value in using this layered (nesting) bowl thinking is that the board leads the organization by simply defining the broadest policies the organization can interpret, understand, and use. This principle can help the board escape immense detail.

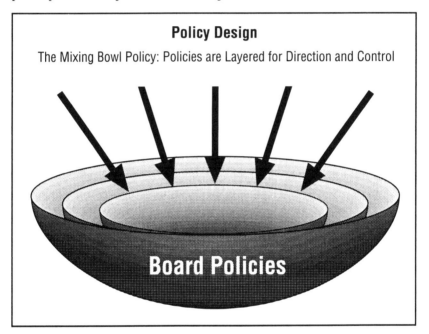

Policy Design

The Mixing Bowl Policy: Policies are Layered for Direction and Control

Board Policies

Governance Model Assumptions

The Board Is in Charge

The organizational model is developed with the assumption that the board of directors is to be the central body of the organization and that it is responsible for setting policy and establishing the fundamental keys to a successful organization. The board is in charge. Against this backdrop, the board must be responsible for setting organizational policy in areas that best communicate to the overall organization.

Values and Vision Are Fundamental to Leadership

The organizational model includes a policy cog that is based on leading with values and vision. The board should capture its values and vision in carefully constructed policy statements that guide the organization. It sometimes is difficult to get all board members excited about this "policy thinking," but this is a vital component of leadership success. The term "policy" can conjure thinking of bureaucratic, hard-to-read documents written in legalese or King James language. However, policy may be defined simply in a new way that is meaningful, concise, and comprehensive. Policy can be defined as a documented communication of the board that establishes a framework for vision, values, and organizational authority and expectations. For example, governance model policies do the following:

- Define the long-term vision of the future.
- Clarify the board's role and the roles of subordinate groups.
- Proactively specify decision making on board-level issues.
- Empower the organization by establishing boundaries of acceptable activity rather than defining all the numerous and infinite possibilities of "how to" policies.

Detail Is Not Board Work

The goal of good governance is to free the board from dealing with detail-type decisions that are best made by subordinate groups. Boards never meet for long enough periods to accomplish all that must be done to totally perform the activities of the organization, so it is critical that the board deal with the right things during its meeting time. Properly delegating appropriate decision making can allow the organization to be more productive and responsive to change. It also can take the board out of a parental, approval mode so that it has more time to devote to direction setting and carving out the future—providing strategic leadership.

A turning point for one board came when it realized there were forty-seven agenda items scheduled for a four-hour meeting. It's no wonder the board members were frustrated. For a room full of board members to have meaningful discussion on forty-seven items in four hours is impossible. Members of this board found they were rubber stamping proposals to finish the meeting—even on overtime. Rubber stamping is a significant waste. It wastes board member talent by not providing an opportunity to tap leader wisdom. And, it wastes time. Furthermore, rubber stamping can be a demotivator for board members and others. There are many cases where board involvement isn't adding value to the decision-making process. All this contributes to board member dissatisfaction.

Board Work Must Add Value

Another key assumption is that the board of directors should do work only where the outcomes offer added value to the organization. Therefore, policy should serve as a guide for the board to define what decisions are board-level issues. Policy must itself contain responses to "what are board-level issues?" When a board hasn't defined what it considers to be board-level issues, it leaves open the question for anyone in the organization to determine what these issues are. It leaves the organization to somehow determine which decisions are "hot," critical, sensitive, and so on. Without criteria from the board on board-level subjects, member leaders and staff typically will submit board agenda items they consider important. Without a filter for agendas, who is to judge what goes on the agenda? Often, lengthy agendas result because they include all items submitted. Once an item is on the agenda, the board must spend the time to resolve it, whether or not it was a board-level issue. In this atmosphere, valuable time will be spent on issues that are not appropriate for board attention. Additionally, if someone chooses to eliminate a proposed item, it can foster hard feelings among board members, which detracts from the unity that is so important for boards.

Definitions of board-level issues and decision-making authority should be written explicitly as policies of the board. It is through written policy, and ultimately communication of that policy to the organization, that subordinate groups know what is expected and what is not. Once board-level issues are stated, subordinate groups can be empowered and free to implement what the board already has said would be approved. In effect, the board, through the use of the governance model, can preapprove the vital happenings in the organization. Effective boards, through proactive policy, predefine actions that are expected from the organization.

Policy Is Vital

One key function of the board is to create policy. Policies can be grouped into policy types and must encompass all board policies. These policy types can be used to construct a concise, usable policy manual.

It is helpful to recognize where board policy resides in the hierarchy of documents. Board policy is so key to the future success of an organization that it is subordinate only to the purpose, articles of incorporation, and bylaws. It is important that board policy documents have high visibility in the working environment of the organization because these documents are especially important to lead and guide the subordinate organization. Broad communication of board policy is necessary.

Where are the policies of your organization? Often, board documents are stored in various places under various names. To find past board policies, an exhaustive search may be required. Ultimately, they may be found in procedures, guidelines, rules, regulations, actions, decisions, and minutes, all of which pose as board policy. These pseudo policies often capture board policy in various formats and become buried and out of sight from the board and the organization.

Good Governance Signifies an Effective Board

Good governance signifies an effective board, and an effective board demands good governance. The two terms "good governance" and "effective board" are synonymous. It is impossible to have one without the other. Good governance means the board is performing in a productive and effective role for the strength and empowerment of the organization. An effective board means that good governance is being applied to all aspects and strata of the organization.

How would you like to be a new board member trying to understand the background for the new job on your board? Often, board members serve three-year terms or less. In these years, the policies of past decisions often will be largely forgotten or unknown. One board member said, "It took me the entire three years to understand my role as a board member, and now I'm gone." This board member knew the frustration of trying to learn about the role of a board member, and it took three years. Then this person observed a new board member who, at the end of the first board meeting, experienced the same glazed-eye look of wonderment that he remembered of himself earlier.

However, with good governance, incoming board members will be able to contribute as effectively as tenured board members. It should not be uncommon for new board members to participate as comfortably, creatively, and effectively as any seasoned member of the board. With a good governance system in place, an observer of a board meeting should find it impossible to detect a first timer from an experienced board member, based on participation and involvement. Who does most of the talking at board meetings can be a tell-tale sign of the strength or weakness of your governance system. Good governance will yield the broadest participation from the full range of board members—independent of their experience on the board. Good governance allows boards to build on member strengths and reduce personal involvement barriers.

Chapter 2

Characteristics, Job Products, Expectations, and Responsibilities of an Effective Board

Definition of an Effective Board

An effective board has a vision and an overall view of just what an effective board really is. Few people have experienced an effective board, so just how would you recognize one if you saw it?

The key to recognizing an effective board is understanding its definition and recognizing its characteristics. Here is a definition of an effective board that can challenge your expectations:

An effective board is a board that leverages diversity and teamwork to foster and propagate an empowered organization for optimum progress toward the vision by skillfully conducting undiluted good governance, through creating vision, writing policy, monitoring progress, and leading, while upholding strong principles of consensus, cooperation, unity, trust, respect, teamwork, and communication.

Characteristics of an Effective Board

An effective board will manifest the definition offered earlier and will exhibit several key characteristics. The following are eleven characteristics of an effective board:

1. **A Clearly Defined Role**—An effective board will know its job. Its role will be documented clearly in board policy, and that role will be reviewed annually, sometimes modified,

and always adopted so each board member, new or not, can claim clear ownership of his or her board position.

2. **Leadership**—An effective board will exhibit leadership to the breadth and depth of the organization. It is this exhibited leadership that turns the cogs of policy, people, and provisions to ensure the organization's success.

3. **Knowledge of Their Governance Process**—An effective board will know and understand good governance. It will know all about its purpose, roles, and job products. In addition, board members will be looking continually for ways and means to further implement good governance throughout their subordinate groups and throughout the organization and staff. Effective board members accept training and, in some cases, serve as trainers for others.

4. **Attention to Policy Matters**—An effective board always will be about matters of policy. Rather than becoming misdirected by focusing on plans and detailed actions, the board will be centering on policy refinement and policy clarification while broadly monitoring the organization's progress toward the vision.

5. **High Regard for People**—An effective board will have high regard for people. Members of the board, members of the organization, and members of the staff all should be seen as valuable partners—all acting as stakeholders contributing to the success of the organization.

6. **Understanding Organizational Provisions**—An effective board will have enough breadth of understanding of the financial structure and operational foundations to be successful. The board should not trifle in the details of day-to-day operations, but should permit broad delegation and the spirit of empowerment.

7. **Governance Task Orientation**—An effective board will understand the role of the board and focus attention on the tasks of governance, not the actions and duties of subordinate groups and staff.

8. **Customer and Total Quality Focus**—An effective board will have a total quality focus, with an eye toward meeting customers' needs.
9. **Flexibility to Adapt to Change**—An effective board always will exhibit flexibility to adapt to the rapidly moving change that is ever escalating. Boards must learn quickly, respond, and be focused on the future rather than be bound to the past.
10. **High Ethical Standards**—An effective board will operate with high ethics and document appropriate values as limitations for the organization. The board must expect operations to abide by stated values and legal standards. It must provide appropriate discipline when required.
11. **Success Celebrations**—An effective board will find reasons to celebrate its successes. As accomplishments are tracked and completed, an effective board will augment feelings of success for every member by celebrating its successes as a team.

Expectations for the Board

Boards can be very busy about the wrong things. Often, the board may be focusing on internal items of seeming importance (but that really should be delegated), listening to lengthy reports of organizational feedback, and not spending time in the area most important for the organization. An effective board needs to be busy about board business. Good governance helps solve this problem.

The board of directors needs to have a clear vision and long-range direction for the organization, along with a method to document and communicate this direction. The board must articulate the direction for the organization so all concerned can be knowledgeable about the organization. If the board doesn't do this, then the organization is relegated to swimming, usually aimlessly, in a sea of ideas, opportunity, and change without causing the organization to move toward a common good—the good that the organization exists to accomplish. An effective board needs to have and communicate vision. Good governance helps solve this problem.

Often, the board underutilizes its potential. Typically, individual board members are talented, capable, and full of exciting expertise, but often these same board members are so underutilized that the board exhibits a vivid waste of valuable member resources. Too often the board underutilizes member potential by rubber stamping recommendations of committee work and staff and ends up working on endless short-term matters that ultimately have little consequence to the common good of the organization. An effective board needs to fully use all board member potential. Good governance helps solve this problem.

Key Job Products and Responsibilities of the Board

One of the purposes of the governance model is to provide a visible place for policy to document the expectations and responsibilities of the board of directors. In the governance model, these are expressed as job products of the board. The job products of the board of directors of any organization can be as numerous or as few as decided by the board itself. What is important is that job products be documented so all current and incoming board members quickly can be aware of the job requirements and expectations. Board policy is the ideal place to fairly define and document what those key job products are. Although every board should come to grips with its customized list, here is a sample list that has broad application and can be used as a starting point.

1. **Write Board Policies.** The key and most fundamental of all job products of the board of directors of any organization is to write policy. This means to craft, prepare, document, communicate, and keep revisiting policy to establish the organizational policy as the best it can be for the organization. It means crafting policy in all four areas of governance for the organization.

2. **Ensure Organizational Performance.** Just as the board of directors establishes the vision for the organization, monitoring is required to ensure headway is being made. Monitoring can validate that the organization is, in fact, making progress toward the stated vision. The board of directors ultimately must be responsible for the well being of the organization, therefore the board must be sufficiently aware of progress (or lack of it) so that appropriate corrective measures can be taken as necessary and only when required.

3. **Provide Leadership.** The board, by definition, is the initiating leadership of the organization. If the board doesn't start the leadership, then nobody else likely will—but if somebody else does, then beware because the board is in for more trouble than it can conceive. The board needs to be the up-front visible leader for a powerful, directed, outward-looking, and progressive organization.

4. **Administer the Nomination and Election Processes.** Some part of the organization must be responsible for the assurance of continuity and successful personnel progression. The board should maintain ownership of this process to provide leadership for the future through carefully selected officers. This is a typical job product of the board of directors. A current board is in the best position to propagate the future board for the benefit, vitality, and success of the whole organization. So, one of the key job products of the board of directors should be establishment of election rules, guidelines, and procedures for the selection of future board members and officers. Similar information is required for filling vacancies, as required.

5. **Implement Effective Governance.** Another job product of the board of directors is to create, document, and implement effective governance for the whole of the organization. It is important that the entire organization, including subordinate groups and staff, be aware of and understand the philosophies and processes of governance being used by the board.

6. **Clarify Subordinate Group Roles and Responsibilities.**
   Successful organizations need to be able to create, organize, and manage expanded facets of the organization. One of the job products of the board of directors should be to establish the organizational and structural makeup of subordinate groups of the organization. The board should document this organizational structure through board policy.

7. **Conduct Effective Board Meetings.** The board of directors of any organization is established to provide leadership and management to the organization. Because the board of directors, by definition, involves a group of people, it means these people need to come together in meetings or electronic media to perform their business. These business meetings allow opportunities to exercise team growth, while working to gain concurrence on key issues. The board should be creating an environment for positive progress toward accomplishing the purposes of the organization.

8. **Select, Support, and Evaluate the Chief Staff Officer.**
   Even the smallest organizations usually have a chief staff officer. One of the key job products of the board of directors is to identify the chief staff officer—the person who will deal with the employment and personnel business of creating a staff to help accomplish the purposes of the organization. The board, in effect, has only one employee—the chief staff officer. All other employees work for and report to the chief staff officer. The board should not meddle in the business of performing detailed performance appraisals or the business of hiring subordinate staff. This is the responsibility of the chief staff officer and his or her staff organization. The board's job is to manage the hiring of the chief staff officer and the annual performance evaluation of the chief staff officer.

Some organizations have implemented the 360-degree performance appraisal system. With this system, input is requested from first-level staff (those reporting to the chief staff officer), from board members plus other key members and leaders, and from the chief staff officer. The president then plays a key role in assembling the input and clearing consensus with the board or its designated subteam, before the actual performance appraisal with the chief staff officer.

Other Board Responsibilities

In addition to the job products discussed earlier, there are several other responsibilities that could be options for a board of directors. These include the following:

- Ensuring proper controls and responsibilities
- Determining the organization's mission and purpose
- Raising money
- Ensuring effective fiscal management
- Engaging in specific strategic planning
- Orienting new board members
- Understanding the relationship between board and staff
- Enhancing the organization's public image
- Organizing itself so it operates efficiently
- Ensuring sound risk-management policies
- Ensuring proper controls and accountability

Every board needs to finalize its list of pertinent job products. In some ways, these additional and expanded job products could be viewed as subsets of the eight key job products of the board of directors as described earlier. Whatever the case, it is important for each board to decide what items are relevant for the board. Job products that are determined to be relevant and pertinent to the whole board should be documented in board policy.

Chapter 3

Establish Vision

ENDs Policies

The first of the four policy categories—ENDs policies—begins with the vision and focuses on the long-term desired outcomes and results. The board's primary job is to set long-term strategic direction. This direction must be captured in the vision and documented in the ENDs policies. ENDs are not services or activities or any means-related functions; they are outcomes, products, impacts, or benefits of those means-related activities. ENDs policies are vectored vision policies—they are externally focused. They answer the following questions:

- What good? (What is the desired outcome?)
- For whom? (Which external customers will this good ultimately serve?)
- What cost? (What amount or percentage of resources does the board place on this desired outcome?)

The vision statement of Alabama Electric Cooperative, Inc., is an excellent example of ENDs language. Its vision is "an economical and reliable power supply for our members through purchase, generation, and transmission of electric energy." This is a vision that deals with external things of what good (economical and reliable power supply) and for whom (our members). In this case, "at what cost" is not mentioned.

Another example of ENDs language is the vision statement of the American Management Association: "Educational forums worldwide where members and their colleagues learn superior, practical business skills and explore best practices of world-class organizations through interaction with each other and expert faculty practitioners." This vision deals with external things of what good (educational forums worldwide) and for whom (members).

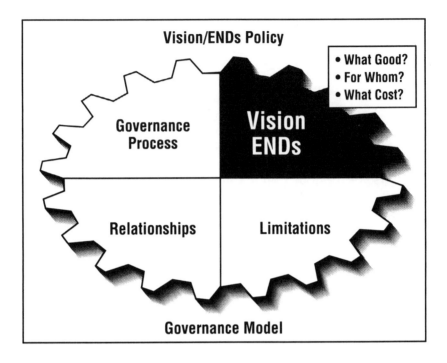

It is vital for a board to establish the vision (a broad ENDs statement) for the organization, identify a few clarifying ENDs for additional direction and definition, then continue to reexplore the ENDs policies on an ongoing basis for improving the vectored vision, direction, and communications. The board may choose to establish further inner ENDs statements of policy (layers) as desired and needed for clarification to members and staff. Each policy may have multiple inner layers of policy as demonstrated by the mixing bowl principle described earlier. ENDs policy statements should continue to be improved, developed, and refined until the board is comfortable accepting any reasonable interpretation by subordinate groups and staff who are responsible for implementing actions to move toward the vision. It is well worth the effort to get comfortable with this powerful ENDs language thinking so these concepts can be implemented.

Importance of Visioning

What is a vision? Visions are not fantasies or nightmares or ethereal supernatural miracles, even though some would tell you that it takes near supernatural effort to develop visions. Vision involves what can be called "a sense of sight," or understanding and wisdom. Visions help to focus a direction targeted at least three to five years (or even ten years) out.

Visions unleash the senses for examining the future and creating a healthy awareness about what can be. Knowing about visions, what they are, and why they are important is just the beginning of understanding. Winners don't win by accident. Winners have a vision. A vision is like a compass. At a glance, the vision points north and shows orientation and direction for which way to go. A vision is like an anchor. It holds steady and prevents drifting from the winds of tempting distractions. A vision is like a rudder. It helps hold the course and avoid either collisions on the rocks of diversions or collisions with other vessels, whether friend or foe. A vision is like a rubber band. The farther it is stretched, the greater the tension. A vision is like a magnet. It attracts otherwise irrelevant ideas and draws in hidden opportunities. A vision is like a radio tower. It transmits intelligent and dependable signals for guidance and control when all else is up for grabs. A vision is like beauty afar. There is incentive to move closer.

Visions are created through a process called visioning. Visioning can be an exciting, successful, and perhaps new experience. Because visioning is a process that involves thinking outside of normal lines of day-to-day interaction, it challenges people to use their creativity and to dream. Creative thinking must be brought to the surface and used to ensure original, innovative, yet realistic, input to successfully view or picture the new and desired future state.

Visioning is picturing a positive, upward, outward, and future-oriented state. It begins with imagination and conceptual descriptions and observations of the mind's eye. As internal energy is focused on understanding, the vision starts to become clearer and clearer. With some effort at documenting the vision, this image of the future can become real and believable. Visioning, then, can be defined simply as the process of picturing an ideal and unique future state—a future state that provides both direction and stretch. A vision is not just a direction; it also is a destination. Although a vision should be believable and realistic, it may or may not be achieved fully. The value is in having an ideal. A vision serves as the ideal, the model, and the destination to be sought after by all. Furthermore, while a vision should be relatively stable, as progress is made, the visioning process should be reemployed to occasionally reshape and sharpen the vision into a better one.

Dreams for the future should be based on current known beginnings. By exploring and documenting expectations of the future state, the gap between the current and the future state will become more tangible. Once the gap is perceived, then work can become more dedicated, focused, and progressive. A strategic plan can be determined to chip away at consciously crossing the gap. Each step of moving pass obstacles in the gap provides movement a little closer toward the reality of what is envisioned in the desired future state.

Visioning means looking ahead and conceptualizing a realistic stretch view of the future. It means comparing the current state with a desired state. The desired state should describe an achievable panorama of growth. Visioning is for leaders who want to move beyond their current state to a more desirable, but not yet existing, future state. Visioning is for people who can imagine a new and better future state and who want to achieve beyond what they currently have experienced. Visioning is an acquired capability of an effective board.

Visioning—An Analogy

Visioning is vital for future successes. Because there are no assurances about the challenging path to the future, there is always uncertainty and risk. However, the risk is worth it on the road to a desired vision. Visioning is the selection of that special desired destination (vision). The journey is the trip to be taken along various highways to reach the vision. The vehicle used for the journey consists of all acquired knowledge, skills, and resources. The twists and turns along the way are the questions that must be answered to reach the destination. The signs beside the road are the visible ideas and indicators that come to consciousness to tell of warnings and hints of desired actions along the journey. The road map is the strategic plan that identifies the roads expected to be traveled and the actions targeted for accomplishment. Road blocks that show up are critical issues that must be addressed to find ways pass them.

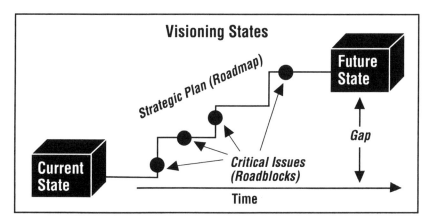

The journey toward a vision can be an exciting experience. Good leaders are able to convey and spontaneously kindle this spirit of adventure. Self-motivating desire stimulates voluntary support and involvement by others and promotes optimum progress toward the desired vision.

With a good vision and sufficient tools—teams and treasures as shown in the engineered organizational model—great things can be accomplished. A good vision can add great value, increase efficiency, and help people get involved to actively work together toward the anticipated desired future. There is no substitute for a good vision for organizations to become efficient.

Qualities of Visions

Vision statements should be clear, inspiring, and concise descriptions of future destinations. They should answer what it will be like and what good will be provided for which recipients as a result of what is done. Vision statements should have certain qualities. Visions should be the following:

- **Future-Oriented**—Visions should be forward looking. They should describe a future destination (not just a direction) and involve a projection at least three to five years (or even ten years) ahead.
- **Inspirational**—One of the functions of leadership is to motivate all those supporting the organization. One special way leaders demonstrate leadership is by inspiring others, especially with an inspiring vision for the future.
- **Clear**—Vision statements should be as clear as possible. Clarity aids understanding.
- **Concise**—Vision statements should be brief.
- **Challenging**—Vision statements should picture a future state that involves some stretch to achieve. If they are too simple or too easily achieved, people will not be challenged.
- **About Excellence**—Visions should build an expectation for the future. They need to be about improvement and excellence.
- **Believable**—Visions should make sense in the marketplace. They should stress flexibility and execution, yet stand the test of time in a turbulent world of change.
- **Broad**—Vision statements need to be broad enough for widespread application throughout the entire organization.
- **Stable but Ever-Challenged**—Vision statements must be stable, but constantly challenged by the board. An effective board should settle for no less than the strongest vision and ENDs statements that have passed through the fires of heated deliberations and found meaning throughout the organization.

- **Empowering to People**—Visions should be empowering to people—members, staff, customers, and all those who are involved with the purpose of the organization.
- **A Guide for Routine Decision Making**—Effective visions provide a dependable guide for logical decision making. When all else is up for grabs, the vision provides helpful definition about which way to go.

Vision Statement Do Nots

Effective vision statements have features that are common for understanding and overall success. They avoid pitfalls that cause problems and shortcomings in communication. The following are some "do nots" for vision statements:

- **No Means**—Vision statements should not describe what actions or means-related activities will be done. Vision statements should address ENDs—what difference will be made for which beneficiaries. ENDs deal with external good.
- **No Action Verbs**—Use of action verbs is an indication of means-related thinking, which has no place in the vision or ENDs statements.
- **No Activity Nouns**—Some activity-related nouns at first may seem appropriate, but they have underlying pitfalls. For instance, words such as "education", "program", and "service" signify a type of means rather than an outcome. Even with descriptive adjectives, these still can be vague.
- **No Interim-Type Words**—Words such as "try", "examine", "seek", "appraise", "strive", and "influence" focus on interim effort or activity rather than outcomes. The focus of vision needs to be on the results rather than activities.
- **No Presumptuous Language**—Visions should not include pretentious, cosmetic words that overstate or exaggerate intentions. Fluff phrases may sound lofty, extensive, and glamorous, but they usually are distracting. Simple, clear, concise language is best.

- **No Lack of Focus**—Vision statements sometimes can be too broad or too narrow in focus. They should be realistic and achievable, while still being challenging.
- **No Subordinate Group Visions**—Vision statements should be broad enough to cover the whole rather than just listing multiple individual subordinate group vision statements. For instance, if a board has authority over subordinate boards, then the vision statement should be crafted to be broad and comprehensive enough to account for the overall vision rather than merely compiling the visions of subordinate groups.

It is a good idea to compare your association's vision statements with those of similar organizations. Gathering knowledge and experiences from others can help cultivate skills at crafting vision statements.

ENDs Versus Objectives

The word "ENDs" is used as a special term in the context of governance for defining vision and direction. It can offer a revealing perspective for how to grow an effective organization. The word "objectives" has been consciously set aside as too vague to be useful. The word "objectives" has been applied in management settings since the 1950s and earlier. It has been applied to all kinds of statements, including combinations of ends- and means-related activities. For clarity of vision, then, it is imperative that "ends" be separated from "means." ENDs are valuable for leading a world-class, effective organization.

The separation of ends and means is done purposely because the board's job of defining vision and direction should be done only through ENDs language. ENDs specifically focus on desired outcomes in terms of "what good," "for whom," and at "what cost," without stipulating how it must be done. The organization needs to feel empowered to use the most optimum and efficient ways, means, and methods possible to reach the desired outcome. The concept of separating ends and means maximizes the freedoms of all pertinent people to be empowered to make numerous, timely, customer-focused, means-related decisions. *How* ENDs are achieved is not a job product of the board. This must be determined by those who are working toward the vision.

This powerful common sense principle provides expectations that those closest to the customers and who have the most specific and pertinent knowledge should have the freedom to choose the best means-related activities to maximize progress. They then are able to create, refine, and determine in a timely manner the best "hows" for accomplishing their goals.

ENDs policy statements sometimes can seem lackluster. However, ENDs don't need to be catchy. They *do* need to address what the future looks like and where the organization is going. ENDs are not required to be catchy slogans as long as they are understood by everyone, especially board members and staff leadership, because their role is to make the vision come alive and become real and personal to others throughout the organization.

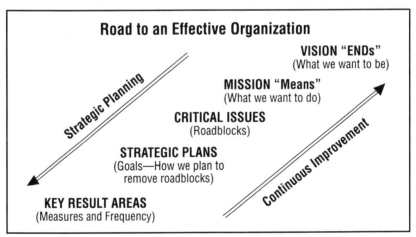

ENDs and Missions

The governance model establishes the ENDs policy language for expressing the highest level vision policy that must respond only to the questions of "what good," "for whom," and at "what cost."

Verbs describing hows are not to be used. Action verbs apply only to means and never to ENDs statements. ENDs statements describe for the organization "what we want to be." A typical vision statement may begin with the phrase, "Our vision is to be (or become)..." with a description of a future state.

Missions are multiple means statements. Therefore, vision and missions statements are different. Missions are not ENDs. Missions statements are not to be part of a policy manual. Missions statements can be part of an organizational plan showing progress needs of the organization. Missions support *how* the vision and ENDs are to be accomplished. Mission statements can define appropriately the hows through the use of action verbs. Action verbs describe methods, responses, practices, and actions, or more generally, the hows—how to make progress toward the vision and ENDs. Missions are activities supported by goals and actions as documented in the strategic plan of the organization. The strategic plan is a vital tool for ensuring progress of the organization. It summarizes established actions and plans created by the subordinate organization and staff and provides the ability to track progress. Visions describe what we want to be and missions describe what we want to do. Visions are ends related and missions are means related. The vision is top level. Missions, actions, and goals define the numerous subordinate activities for moving toward the vision.

Critical Issues

For an organization to make progress, it must determine what the critical issues are. Sometimes it is difficult to pinpoint the problem areas called critical issues. One way to see critical issues, is to think of them as roadblocks. What are the roadblocks that can impede progress toward the vision? Once these roadblocks are listed, they serve as powerful and strikingly useful input for determining pertinent actions of the strategic plan.

Strategic Plan

The strategic plan is an important document for an effective organization. The plan shows the layers of missions, goals, and actions to address the critical issues and ensure progress toward the vision. The strategic plan, in effect, describes how the organization plans to remove the roadblocks to maximize progress toward the vision.

The strategic plan is an appropriate and important tool to help guide the organization and monitor performance. This tool contains a listing of all the missions, goals, and actions the subordinate organization and staff are planning to accomplish in the coming year. These missions, goals, and actions must be created and "owned" by the subordinate organization. The board's job is not to create the strategic plan but to be sure of the existence of the plan so that powerful pride of ownership progress is made toward the vision and direction of the total organization.

Even though the strategic plan is a powerful tool of the organization, the strategic plan is not policy and, therefore, is not a job product of the board. The board should resist the temptation to work on the strategic plan because this quickly will disempower the organization, create monstrous detail on board agendas, and impede and reduce the potential for progress. However, the board should monitor progress and ensure a working process has been established for this strategic plan to be created, managed, communicated, and implemented throughout the organization.

Key Result Areas

It is important for the board to monitor organizational progress. In a not-for-profit organization, this can be challenging as compared with a for-profit company that has the benefit of focus on bottom-line financial measures. The board should establish the key result areas that tell the story of progress (or lack of it). The board should determine the specific measures that best indicate the key results of operations and the frequency with which the board would like to see the results monitored. As the board comes to grips with this monitoring measure and frequency information, the information should be documented in board policy in the relationships segment of the policy manual. This is where all subordinate group and staff roles and expectations are shown. Monitoring information shown in the relationships segment helps to further define the expectations for subordinate groups and staff. Note that the board can create benchmarks based on these monitoring results. The board must define the vision and track key result areas of progress toward that vision.

Mind the Goals and Actions for Progress

The board should have the job product of writing board policy for the vision and direction of the organization. The board cannot single-handedly accomplish, over the coming year, all the desired actions toward that vision—that is why subordinate groups and staff exist. It is healthy for the board to be aware that the strategic plan exists not only for use by the subordinate groups and staff, but that the plan has relative substance to goals, actions, and plans. This should be considered part of the monitoring function of the board (which is a board job product). Managing the strategic plan is not board business, but monitoring is.

Examples of Vision Policies

An example of a vision statement is the vision of the Illinois Farm Bureau. It reads: "The economic well-being of agriculture and the quality of farm family life."
- "What good" is answered: The economic well-being of agriculture and the quality of farm family life.
- "For whom" is defined: Farm families.
- "At what cost" is not stated.

A vision statement that responds to any or all of these areas is an ENDs statement. ENDs policies deal with these three simple, powerful questions that are reserved for the board to answer: what good, for whom, and at what cost.

Another example of an ENDs policy comes from the Society of Automotive Engineers (SAE). The vision of SAE is "the advancement of the mobility community to serve humanity." This ENDs policy answers "what good" (advancement of the mobility community) and "for whom" (humanity), but the statement is very broad and could be misinterpreted. More detailed ENDs definitions in SAE's policy manual help to clarify the vision for the organization so any reasonable interpretation can be applied. In this case, the vision statement finishes with the word "including" and several following statements help to clarify the vision statement. For example, one of the inner layers of clarification states, "A worldwide network of technically informed mobility practitioners." This answers "what good" (worldwide network) and "for whom" (technically informed mobility practitioners).

The vision of Levi Strauss is "a company that our people are proud of and committed to, where all employees have an opportunity to contribute, learn, grow, and advance based on merit, not politics or background." The statement is focused internally. Although the statement includes a good sense of values concerning employees, the reason they're in business (what good) has not been addressed. Visions should be focused on meeting external customer needs (what good, for whom, at what cost).

Vision or Mission?

Appendix A is a quiz for evaluating vision and mission statements. Many of the vision and mission statements in this appendix are mentioned in Graham and Havlick's *Mission Statements*. For those interested in crafting their own vision and mission statements, this exercise can be useful for understanding the principles involved. The questions allow you to practice the application of ENDs and means thinking as applied respectively to visions and missions.

Chapter 4

Define the Governance Process

Governance—Board Business

The governance process—or operations policy—is the first of the three means segments of policy. Governance process policies are extremely important in building an effective board. These policies document the philosophy and style of governance to be used by the board. They define how the organization is governed, officer roles and responsibilities, and the job products of the board. The way the board conducts itself is inherently a model for the rest of the organization. Therefore, the methods of operation selected and used by the board always influence subordinate groups (either positively or negatively). They become a pattern for subordinate groups and staff to emulate.

Governance Process Policies

Governance process policies describe the board's values concerning the process of governance and how the board will govern the entire organization. They provide leadership responses to fundamental issues of vision, values, authority, and roles. Governance process policies establish, for the board and the whole organization, the chosen philosophy of governance and describe the style of operations to be used. Good governance, as defined by board policy, should characterize and communicate the board's shared expressions of values. Board governance process policies should state that board policies will be communicated through documented policies in all four major policy segments. The governance process segment also includes descriptions of the roles and responsibilities or position descriptions of the key officers of the organization. In addition, governance process policies define accountability and specifics of job products of the board itself.

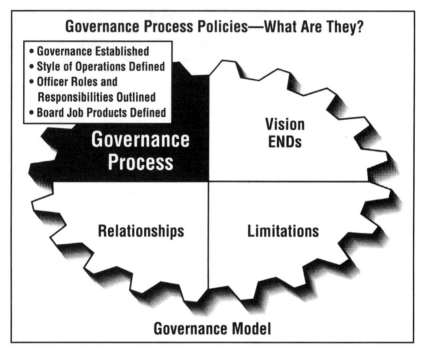

Governance Process Policies—What Are They?

- Governance Established
- Style of Operations Defined
- Officer Roles and
  Responsibilities Outlined
- Board Job Products Defined

Governance Process

Vision ENDs

Relationships

Limitations

Governance Model

Governance policies are an important area for the board because board members will continue to be unclear about roles of officers, and even their own role as a board member, until it is defined. Without clear definition of these roles, responsibilities, and job product expectations, it is common for retiring board members to come to the end of their term and say how difficult it was to measure whether or not their personal contribution was worthwhile and successful. The governance model specifically contains this mandatory, but often overlooked, governance process segment to create a place for the board to establish its own expectations for the board and broadly define how the organization is to be governed.

Clarify and Document Job Products of the Board

The governance process policy segment is the place not only to define how the board governs the organization, but it also is the place to clarify the role of the board. Too often, a board assumes that board members know what they are to do. Some members will say, "My job as a board member is to come to the meetings and comment on the issues at hand." This narrow and limiting attitude often is surrounded by noble motives and desires. It is a waste for a board not to use to the fullest extent its dedicated, hard-working, knowledgeable, and willing members because they have no idea what their overall role as board member is.

The board owes it to its members to clarify the members' roles by defining and documenting the expected results of their work. This role clarification as documented in policy language is called "job products." Job products are the desired outcomes, expectations, and results, including products, services, processes, or functional requirements, that support the purpose of the organization. A key governance process policy, therefore, should be developed to visibly define the specific job products of the board itself.

As a matter of mechanics, the job products of the board of directors should be documented in the governance process segment of governance policy because this is where the board shows how it will govern. All groups subordinate to the board also should have documented job products, but these job products (defined and assigned by the board) should be shown in the relationships policies, where the board establishes the total organizational structure.

Job Products of the Board

As described in detail in chapter two, there are eight job products with which many boards need to deal. Some boards will add other elements to its own job product lists, and other boards will arrive at a shorter list. Every board should spend time to determine its own expectations by working through its list of particular job products that describe its expectations for board accomplishments.

Job Products of the Board

1. Write board policies
2. Ensure organizational performance
3. Provide leadership to the organization
4. Administer the nomination and election processes
5. Implement effective governance
6. Clarify subordinate group roles and responsibilities
7. Conduct effective board meetings
8. Select, support, and evaluate the chief staff officer

Once an organization has adopted the governance model, including the governance process policies, extensive training and orientation must be conducted on an annual and ongoing basis. Each transition of outgoing and new incoming board members creates a brand new board. Each new board must be oriented and trained about its roles and responsibilities. The new board should begin with the framework developed by its predecessor, then set out from that basis for continuous improvement for the future. Before the organizing session for the new board, all the board members should have had sufficient training and orientation so that all members will be able to start off with a strong background and knowledge base.

Role of the President

Governance process policy is the place to document the defined role for each of the major officers of the organization, including the president, treasurer, secretary, and any other positions the board decides are needed.

The role of the elected president, for instance, begs definition. Every board should spend time to define expectations for the person who fulfills the role of president. In the policy describing the role of president, some expectations may include, for example, that the president take an active role in board meetings as chairperson to ensure integrity of the board's governance processes and to ensure the board behaves consistent with its own policies. The president may be expected to take an active role in preparing board agendas through active listening, with wide input from various sources, and to exercise wisdom for interpreting and applying board policy. The president may be expected to make good decisions concerning the appropriate tasks related to the board's own work by using policy as the filter for board agendas. The president may be expected to appoint various individuals to the subordinate groups, including various boards, subteams, committees, and all other functional groups of the organization. The president also may be expected to serve as the official spokesperson of the organization.

Board Member Responsibilities

Governance process policy is the place to document policy regarding board member responsibilities. What exactly are the responsibilities of board members? Board members should expect of themselves a certain mature component of loyalty to the interests of the membership. This can be described as a commitment to a standard of behavior as documented in the board member responsibility policy. Board members should do the following:

- Support and defend board policies
- Promote a climate of trust, respect, and teamwork
- Avoid personal conflicts
- Be diligent in preparing for and attending meetings
- Maintain relationships of cooperation
- Plan the annual agenda of the board

Support and Defend Board Policies

Whatever the organization is about, all the individual board members should be projected as champions and leaders. Any policies adopted by the whole board should be supported and defended by all the leaders, officers, and board members who have the power to establish or change policies.

The job of the board is to deal with the cutting-edge issues affecting the organization; therefore, board members should be communicating on policy improvements. Occasionally, board members are tempted outside the board room to project a posture at odds with current policy. This is not acceptable. Individual board members are expected to provide pertinent and knowledge-based input for deliberations to nurture continuing policy improvement for the organization. However, board members should resist attitudes of being at odds with current policy outside the board room in a derogatory, demeaning way, where there is no real way of effecting a policy change at the time. Board members are obliged to support and defend existing policies. Listening and learning about customer input and needs for the future and projecting a spirit of continuous improvement for the benefit of all is not nearly as difficult as some would say. There is a distinct difference in attitude between the person who is badmouthing current policy versus the person who is striving for policy improvements based on the values, purposes, and ideals of the organization.

Promote a Climate of Trust, Respect, and Teamwork

Individual board members should be expected to promote a climate of trust, respect, and teamwork. There are many styles of working together, but at the root of a good working relationship of a board of directors is trust and respect. It is a good idea to monitor the levels of trust by including a pertinent question about this on the meeting survey at the end of each board meeting. Then plot the progress.

As shown in Appendix E (Board Inventory Assessment), several questions can help evaluate the progress of the board in several areas. One of those questions relates to trust. Usually this shows a high influence in the decision-making process. In the board inventory assessment form under decision making, the assessment is shown on a scale from zero to six, ranging from accomplishments taking total priority over trust and respect versus trust and respect taking total priority over tangible accomplishments of the hour. Annual evaluation of key board qualities, such as trust, can be monitored through this board inventory assessment tool. Once the assessment has been performed, it is important that board members see the results and have opportunity to build and make progress.

Teamwork is an acquired skill, and people will exhibit varying levels of teaming abilities. It always is a pleasure to see a true master of teamwork indirectly teaching the skill and molding the thinking of the board on given issues through open teaming interaction. This cooperative ability can be fostered and learned through a natural growing process with personalized refinements along the way.

Avoid Personal Conflicts

Board members should be expected to remain free of conflicts of interest. If the board desires to establish more detailed limitations for board members, this can be done, but individual board members should not become affiliated as agents or representatives of companies or organizations that could cause conflicting decisions in the board room.

Be Diligent in Preparing for and Attending Meetings

Board members can be effective as teaming members of the board only if they are present at meetings. It also is true that diligent preparation will be helpful for individual members who expect to be most effective in the role of a team player. Making attendance records visible to the board at each meeting makes everyone aware of the status of attendance. An effective board can be achieved only by building on the consistent interdependent strengths of all the board members.

Maintain Relationships of Cooperation

One responsibility of the board is to maintain relationships of cooperation inside and outside the organization. For example, it can be helpful to document a policy of external cooperation before a spirited discussion about a sister organization viewed by some as a competitor or rival. The spirit of cooperation is an effective way to ensure growth and to support numerous gains for the benefit of all.

Plan the Annual Agenda of the Board

One of the key job responsibilities of the board is to plan its annual agenda. The board should document expectations for governance tasks for the year. For example, the board should plan its own annual agenda during the organizing session at the first board meeting of the year. Predetermined, documented board governance process policy should state that the annual agenda is to include the organizing tasks. The following five categories are appropriate for an agenda:

1. Develop and revisit ENDs policy.
   - Which new ones are needed?
   - Which policies need clarification and improvements?
2. Monitor organizational performance toward the vision.
   - Are monitoring policies sufficient?
   - Should monitoring goals be established or modified?
3. Revisit appropriate and pertinent means policies.
   - Which policies should be developed for clarification?
   - Which policies should be amended or clarified?
4. Implement the board's governance process.
   - What are the plans for board training?
   - What other governance tasks are needed?
5. Review incidental information.
   - What routine board actions are needed?

A scoreboard can be developed at the organizing session to help define expectations for the coming year and to provide a road map for progress. This also may be a helpful tool the board can use to keep track of its successes to celebrate the results and gain personal satisfaction for the whole board.

Governance Model Policies Serve as a Filter for Agendas

The full complement of board policies ultimately serves as a filter for determining which items are appropriate for the board agenda. Any agenda item must involve one of the four broad segments of board policy; otherwise, it is not board business. Governance process policies should describe how all board agenda items relate to one of these four simple segments of board business.

Governing Style

Governance process policies may include policies such as the governing style the board wishes to use for conducting business. This may include style elements, such as how the board will treat diversity, teamwork, discipline, participation, total quality, and communication.

One significant governance process policy adopted by the Society of Automotive Engineers board was: "Consensus will be sought for decisions put before the board. Board members will have an opportunity to present their views." A translation of this policy is: No more rubber stamping! As a result of this policy, the board's agendas became organized with fewer agenda items, but the items that were included on the agendas had broad impact. Board members are able to spend more time on important agenda items to understand and truly support their decisions. Board members feel greater responsibility for the organization and receive a greater sense of accomplishment for contributing to the success of the organization.

Poor governance involves rifling through topics, with decisions brought to a formal vote with ayes and nays. Dominant, assertive members may express their views and sometimes intimidate others. Discussion time may be minimal and rubber-stamping actions too often are the results.

In contrast, under the governance model, consensus action is focused on what is predefined as board business. All nonboard business will have been previously filtered out. Agenda time will be allocated for the board members to hear input, weigh pros and cons, and discuss and deliberate their decisions. At times their process and schedule may include breakout sessions for further gathering of full insights and crafting and comparing drafts of policy language to most favorably affect the purpose of the whole organization. As a result, the output of this type of governance culture can yield valuable and needed new or improved policy as documented clarification for the board itself and ultimately for the benefit of the entire organization.

Timely Leadership—Before and After

Once the governance model is implemented, there is a contrast in thinking, attitudes, and results. Board agendas will have different content, make-up, and character. The approach to governance will be all together different by the board as well as the subordinate organization and staff. The board will feel more satisfied as individuals and as a team, and board members will understand the leader ownership that is theirs.

The decision process will be different. Instead of taking a vote and asking who is in favor and who is against a particular item (which automatically divides the group), the spirit of consensus (not necessarily compromise) will cause stronger deliberation and better responses for the organization. The board will gain a greater sense of purpose, and its role will be clearer than ever before. The organization will be linked to a greater extent with a spirit of empowerment for everyone concerned.

Monitoring the Governance Process

Of the four governance model policy segments, the governance process policy is beneficial and powerful for internal purposes. This segment defines the job products of the board and the roles and responsibilities of the officers and board members.

As the board embarks on an annual agenda of work to be accomplished, it is good to begin with the end in mind. To ensure that the board allots appropriate time for getting its work done and to be able to celebrate resulting successes, it is important to have a method for establishing the plan for governance and tracking the progress of governance tasks. One way to do this is with a scoreboard.

At the organizing session of the new board each year, the board may find it valuable to agree on a draft of a scoreboard for the year. A draft may be crafted from tasks remaining from the previous year with the addition of new proposed important tasks that have been determined to be board business. The new board then should take time at its first meeting and organizing session to review the draft, then modify and personalize the desired governance tasks through teamwork and consensus. The board should agree after each meeting on the remaining governance task items (the scoreboard) for the year.

The scoreboard outlines the governance tasks the board plans to accomplish during the coming year. It makes sense to divide up the scoreboard into the annual agenda portions of predefined board task areas. These should come from the previously defined board job product policy, which may include the following:

- Revisit ends
- Monitor performance
- Revisit means policies
- Implement governance
- Review incidental items

Then for each of these portions, the scoreboard should include columns for listing tasks for each meeting agenda for the year.

The scoreboard is an ever-changing and fluid document. As new governance task needs come up at meetings, the scoreboard can be updated after each meeting to reflect the best thinking and plans of the board.

One valuable purpose of the scoreboard is to track the progress of the board. Accomplished tasks for the year never should be

Scoreboard to Track Governance Tasks of the Board's Annual Agenda				
	Meetings of the Year			
	No. 1	No. 2	No. 3	No. 4
Revisit ENDs				
Monitor Performance				
Revisit Means				
Implement Governance				
Review Incidentals				

removed; they should be checked off. As governance tasks are completed, they can be shown as completed and left on the scoreboard for the entire year so the board can be visually reminded of its hard work and year-to-date accomplishments. This will give rise to feelings of accomplishment and success, which are the foundation for realistic celebrations. Celebrating successes is an important factor for building teamwork and feelings of satisfaction of the board.

The Board Does Tasks—
It Doesn't "Do" Any Actions

The board of directors does not actually *do* any actions toward the completion of the missions, goals, and plans of the organization. This work is all performed as part of the strategic plan by the organization—all nonboard work.

So what does the board do? The board does governance *tasks*. The board does these governance tasks to lead and guide the organization. The board performs tasks of governance that benefit the entire organization.

As shown in the role of an effective board, it has predetermined to be about leadership and governance—not about meddling in the detailed affairs of operations. Effective boards choose to focus on governance tasks to promote the effectiveness of the breadth of the organization. Good governance tasks include key items, such as the following:

- Providing refined detail (an inner layer) to the vision to provide better organizational guidance.
- Changing the relationships policy, for instance, to form and create a new member council to focus on the needs of a growing portion of the membership.
- Devoting significant board time and effort to defining and refining monitoring policy for exactly what metrics are important for the board to measure progress of the organization toward the vision—and when, how, and how often the board wants to have access to these metrics.

The board should keep from being tempted to personally manage staff, make detailed decisions for headquarters operations, guide intimately the chief staff officer, perform detailed actions for staff, and so forth. The board's job products should include the performance of governance tasks only. These are the things board members do as a group, in a unified manner of consensus.

Chapter 5

Organizing Relationships

Relationship Policies

Relationship policies describe how the board delegates power and authority to the organization. They define the structure of the organization. These policies address the roles and expectations of subordinate groups, committees, and staff. They also define the position descriptions of the various officer positions. In addition, they describe the specific metrics for monitoring progress and the frequency that these measurements are to be displayed to the board.

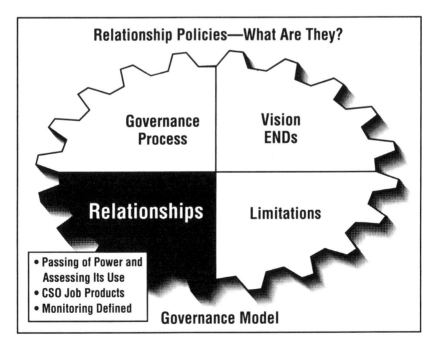

Relationship Policies—What Are They?

Governance Process

Vision ENDs

Relationships

Limitations

- Passing of Power and Assessing Its Use
- CSO Job Products
- Monitoring Defined

Governance Model

Subordinate Groups and Staff

The relationships policy category can be divided into two areas: relationship policies for subordinate member groups that report to the board and relationship policies for the staff side of the organization. The staff of the organization are responsible to the chief staff officer. Therefore, the structure policies addressing staff organization are directed toward the chief staff officer. This approach for writing structure policies in two areas helps to distinguish definitions pertinent to staff from those that pertain to the member side of the organization.

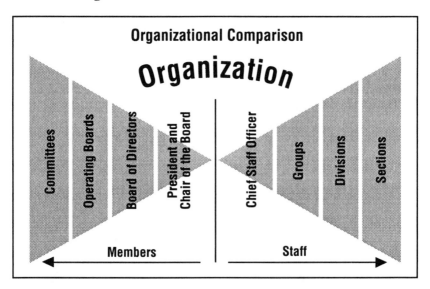

Subordinate Groups Are Accountable to the Board

The broadest relationship policies explain that the subordinate groups and the chief staff officer are accountable to the board and are governed by the policies established by the board. The relationship policies say that the job products of subordinate groups are the achievement of the aims of the organization. These aims are defined in the vision and ENDs shown in board policy. In the board's overall delegation policy statement, the board should remind itself that subordinate groups and staff are authorized to use any reasonable interpretation of board policy. When clarification is needed for the organization, this becomes, by definition, board work.

How to Establish a Subordinate Group

A separate or individualized relationship or structure policy should exist for each subordinate group that reports to the board. The format of these separate structure policies should be simple and consistent to yield a powerful communication tool. To do this, there are three areas that should be addressed for each subordinate group that reports to the board:

1. **Composition**—This is a statement that indicates the make-up of the member group that reports to the board. This includes how many members, who they are (by position, not by the name), term length, from which areas (if important), and so forth.

2. **Scope/Authority**—This statement should describe the decision-making authority of the group. It explains generally what the responsibilities are and specifically what the group is expected to do.

3. **Job Products**—This area of the individualized relationship policies should describe the specific and desired outcomes based on their responsibilities and activities. These can be products, services, or processes. The outcomes should support the ENDs that are expressed in board policy. (Writing policies that describe "what you will stay busy at" should be avoided. Staying busy is not a good aim nor should the level of busyness impress the board. The board should be monitoring the results of what it is busy at for achieving the defined job products. By monitoring these outcomes, the board can and should track the progress toward the vision.)

These three areas of composition, scope, and job products, when defined by the board for each segment of the structure, will pay large dividends. For example, when the organizational structure is clear, projects can be more effectively delegated and expectations can be much more specific, up front, about the kinds of decisions expected. This up-front definition tends to yield more productivity, creativity, and efficiency because confusion is eliminated from the beginning.

An Example of a Relationship Policy

The following is an example of a relationship policy that establishes a finance committee.

Composition: Committee shall consist of the treasurer, assistant treasurer, and eight appointed members, with two members appointed each year for a four-year term.

Scope/Authority: To supervise the financial affairs of the organization. Authorized to buy and sell securities, fixed and other assets, with annual cost less than 10 percent of total net worth. Authorized to approve loans and incur debt not to exceed 25 percent of the total net worth.

Job Products:
- Supervised financial affairs
- Managed annual budgets
- Submitted annual return-on-equity target for board approval
- Maintained financial reports
- Managed loans

In this example, the finance committee is authorized to establish the annual budget consistent with the return-on-equity target, which is approved by the board. Board approval of the budget is not necessary unless the finance committee establishes a budget that is not in line with the return-on-equity target. If this committee has not met board policy, then it must continue to work to meet it or propose a change to board policy.

Don't Take Back Empowerment

Sometimes after the governance model and the policy manual are adopted in an organization, the finance committee, for example, and other subordinate groups in the early stages, inevitably will want to return to the board for various budgetary and operational approvals even though, by policy, they are empowered to make the decisions themselves. There is a natural tendency to revert to the old ways of doing things. Although the strong organization so empowered ultimately will find this new atmosphere refreshing, the transition to this new atmosphere will take training and persistence. This spirit of empowerment allows timely decisions and a faster responding team culture, so don't be tempted to fall back. It is imperative that the board not take back what is has delegated, because this will have a negative effect on empowerment realities that the board is trying to propagate. Empowerment is an attitude of permission and authority to perform actions (within defined limitations) that move the current organization toward the future state as defined in the vision.

Empowerment and accountability go hand-in-hand. It can be comforting to a subordinate group to get board approval, even if it is a rubber-stamp approval, because then the board shares accountability for the potential risk or failure of an initiative.

Staff Report to the Board

The chief staff officer reports to the board; therefore, expectations should be defined in the board relationships policy. There are many benefits to predefining the responsibilities and expectations expressed and documented as job products for the chief staff officer. One special benefit is the visible and documented communication and awareness between the boss and the employee. This has a stabilizing effect on the relationship.

Job Products of the Chief Staff Officer

Job products of the chief staff officer should include these five areas of responsibility:
1. Capability to achieve ENDs of the organization
2. Safety of the assets of the organization

3. Accurate and timely information
4. Favorable public perception of the organization
5. Broad communication internal to the organization

Capability to Achieve ENDs of the Organization—Staff capability means to have staff who are competent and able to achieve the organization's ENDs. Staff, therefore, must be selected carefully in the hiring process, oriented and trained, motivated and encouraged along the way, and ultimately capable of performing. The performance of staff is particularly necessary to accomplish the many goals to provide the products and services expected by the membership. The chief staff officer needs to provide staff and system capability to work toward achieving the vision. In a sense, the chief staff officer is responsible for the people and processes to achieve milestones toward the vision. These people and processes are key resources for an organization to cultivate and grow. This capability is achieved through competency, continuity, continuous improvement, and sound progression and succession plans.

Safety of the Assets of the Organization—System capability relates to protecting the safety of assets and legal status of the organization. The chief staff officer is responsible for proper security, protection, and risk management for the organization. Included are items such as protecting the organization's logo, protecting against misuse of the organization's name, and ensuring no illegal activity. Staff need to police legal abuses as necessary.

Accurate and Timely Information—The chief staff officer should be expected to bring to the board information that is accurate, concise, and pertinent at a frequency and criteria determined by the board. Relevant and timely trends and analyses should be provided along with counsel and appropriate incidental materials to the board and membership.

Favorable Public Perception of the Organization—The chief staff officer should be active in public relations in appropriate areas to establish and maintain favorable perceptions of the organization. Favorable perceptions of the organization can apply to a broad area, but they may be defined as focusing on the key leaders and members and segments that make up the organization, along with pertinent support groups and other stakeholders.

Broad Communication Internal to the Organization— Communications are a key link for the organization, and the chief staff officer should be expected to model the expert communications linkage among all facets internal to the organization. This may include all aspects of communication, from minutes of board meetings to monthly articles in magazines, journals, and periodicals. Some travel may be expected to keep abreast of the membership in various geographical areas—even globally—as required.

Annual goals may be predetermined by the chief staff officer. Having predetermined goals will help facilitate communication with staff and the board and may serve as the basis for the annual performance evaluation. A strong atmosphere of open communications that channels across the breadth and depth of the organization provides untold benefit to all.

Board Predetermines Monitoring Methods

Relationship policies define how the board plans to monitor organizational performance. The board must select key result areas or top-tier critical measures—measures that tell the board whether progress is being made toward the vision and ENDs. Member groups and staff then are responsible for providing regular monitoring data to the board on the selected measures at the frequency specified. It can be helpful to use some standardized reporting process formats for groups to share monitoring data with the board. These predetermined measures of key result areas, along with the standardized reporting process, can improve the efficiency and quality of the board's monitoring process.

As the board comes to grips with monitoring measures and frequency information, this monitoring information should be compiled in board policy in the relationships segment, where all subordinate group and staff roles and expectations are shown.

Showing monitoring information in the relationships segment helps further define expectations for subordinate groups and staff, as benchmarks are established based on the monitoring results.

Key Result Areas

An effective board needs to know whether the organization is (or is not) making sufficient progress toward the vision. To do this, the board should establish the key result areas and determine the specific measures and benchmarks that best indicate the top-tier results of operations. The board also should determine how often it would like these results monitored. A defined focus and process of monitoring, with measures at predetermined frequencies, help communicate what the board thinks is most important. This encourages subordinate groups and staff to monitor these top-tier items plus, inevitably, a host of other, more detailed, but pertinent parameters for their respective areas.

Once effective monitoring is established, the board is in a far stronger position to effect timely corrective action when and if needed. As a result of good monitoring, it is a natural progression to use the historic information to target improvements and establish benchmarking for progress.

As a board becomes more effective, more advanced ideas and methods will surface for applying the skills of powerful knowledge-based decision making. Notice how the implementation of good governance yields a progression of ever-spiraling benefits. These benefits come from a strengthened and effective board yielding a motivated and empowered organization.

Chapter 6

Limitations for Empowerment

Getting Things Done

Boards often are made up of members who are "stars" of the organization, and they want to see the most happen in the shortest time. These stars oftentimes are knowledgeable and informed; they know the methods and solutions the organization should be using. But is this really board business? Remember, the organization is responsible to move toward the vision. The board does the vision setting and governance tasks.

Sometimes even well-intended language from the board to the subordinate organization can be less than ideal. For example, the board can be very busy with *how* to accomplish things that lead to progress for the organization. Now, suppose the board does good work and defines some good how solutions for today's problems. Will those same solutions be effective next year or five years from now? If a board captures a how solution to a problem in minutes, procedures, or policy, then, inevitably, the organization is compelled to live by this how forever—or until the board changes it.

Over time, it becomes impossible for the board to keep defining the how solutions or means of solving all the problems for the organization. This quickly leads to rubber stamping by the board and the spiral of discouragement. It is impossible to always revisit all those previously good answers to be sure they are up to date and effective for the current environment. Therefore, it is important that the board not get caught in the trap of defining the hows.

This is why the board creates an organizational structure in relationships policy to answer these how questions.

A Better Way—Limitations!

What is a better way? A better way is for the board to create organizational structure in the relationships policy, then do the following:
- Define the acceptable limitations on hows in board policy.
- Ensure that appropriate subordinate groups are working the right strategic issues and defining the hows themselves.
- Monitor the macro progress of the organization toward the vision and direction as defined in board policy.

Getting Things Done—The Board Does It?

Does your board ever get into the mode of describing hows for subordinate groups of the organization? It is easy to spend large amounts of time on detailed, specific solutions. Usually, selected board members will begin to champion their solutions, and the board as a whole will have feelings of inadequacy and be dominated by too few people on too many issues to respond well to any of them. Establishing a limitations policy is the solution.

Have you seen subordinate groups always bringing problems, questions, and solutions to the board for its approval? If this happens often, then it is a signal of an ineffective and unempowered organization. If the board becomes saddled with the demanding duty of always being the high-volume, detailed, organizational problem solvers, it soon will become the rubber stamper of the solutions that are drafted somewhere by others in advance of the meeting. This results in feelings of dissatisfaction about board job performance and in dissatisfied board members; it adds time delays to the solutions needed for a world-class organization, and the organization as a whole becomes unempowered to get the job done. Establishing limitations policy is the solution.

What Are Limitations Policies?

Limitations policies establish boundaries and empower subordinate groups and the chief staff officer. Limitations permit subordinate groups and the chief staff officer to use any and all reasonable means to accomplish their respective job products as defined and shown in relationships policy, as long as they are acting within the limitations policy. The board doesn't need to define all the hows—the board puts limitations on the hows used within the organization. With this system, the organization is free and empowered to use any means solutions to make progress and meet customer needs, as long as they are within the limitations. This principle is a strong way to implement and drive empowerment.

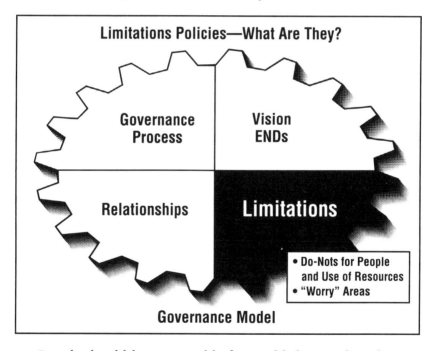

Boards should be responsible for establishing policy that reflects adherence to federal, state, and local laws. Limitations policy can do that. Various abuses in the corporate world could have been prevented if boards had been more visible with limitations. Some examples are described in *Taming the Giant Corporation* by Ralph

Nader. At Gulf Corporation, three successive chief executive officers paid out over $12.6 million in foreign and domestic bribes over a fifteen-year period. At Northrop, the chairperson and vice president created and funded the Economic and Development Corporation, a separate Swiss company, and illegally paid $750,000 to a Swiss attorney to stimulate West German jet sales. At 3M, the chairperson ordered the company insurance program to fraudulently record payments as "necessary and proper" business for tax purposes. And at Ashland Oil, the chief executive officer was involved in illegally generating and distributing $801,165 in domestic political contributions. Boards should clearly define limitations for their organizations to prevent abuse.

Limitations policies define and state the board's values about the practice of operations for the operating groups and staff. When dealing with these policies, the board answers the question: "What practices or circumstances would not be allowed?" This is the board's list of "do nots."

Limitations Policies Are Boundaries in Negative Language

Limitations policies are written using negative language, typically using the word "not". For example, a sentence from a board limitation policy could be: "The organization is 'not' to do anything illegal, imprudent, or unethical."

Initial reaction to the negative language may be negative itself. Some people may be turned off by this policy category, but they need not be. It has exciting potential. Although some view this as a negative way to run things, it can have a strong and positive effect on an organization.

Defining the Unacceptable Permits All Else

When the board describes unacceptable areas for decision making, it is actually shaping what is acceptable. Therefore, with limitations, operating groups and staff are empowered to do what is not prohibited by limitations policy. They are authorized to use any reasonable interpretation of the limitations policy and, therefore, have great freedom. These policies merely establish boundaries for member groups and staff decision making. In other words, if the board hasn't said you *can't* do it, you *can*!

Limitations Policy for Empowerment

Limitations policy is one of the most powerful concepts for mobilizing and empowering an organization. These policies limit only the means. All actions within these limits are acceptable means and are options available to a progressive organization.

An example of a limitations policy is: "The chief staff officer shall not allow or cause any action or decision in his/her area of supervision and control that is imprudent, illegal, unethical, or that detracts from the purpose of the organization." Although some would say the directive is obvious, many boards that have made assumptions about this have run into trouble. In fact, that was the case for United Way, when its chief staff officer was terminated a few years ago.

The United Way Board discovered its chief staff officer had hired several family members and paid them extremely generous salaries, used corporate vehicles and planes to conduct personal business, and abused several other privileges. Lawsuits regarding the case are still in progress. The integrity of United Way's entire business was questioned by the public. People wondered, "Where did my charitable contribution go?" It was a devastating blow to United Way's reputation. A study of the United Way case revealed that the chief staff officer had not violated a single United Way Board policy. The board should have established limitations policy for the chief staff officer along with corresponding relationships monitoring. This would have made boundaries clear, and monitoring would have prevented or revealed early signs of abuse.

Tackle Limitations Policies First

Limitations policies are the board's "worry areas." The board should talk about what it wouldn't put up with, what the penalties would be if a policy were violated, and then translate this into limitations policy. The board should tackle this area first when creating policies. Once the board establishes a first draft of the limitations policy, it is free to think more creatively about other policy segments, such as vision, ENDs, and direction setting.

It's Short Work

Another principle driving the definition of limitations policy is that it would be virtually impossible for a board to write policies about all acceptable actions. One board was operating with a four-foot-high stack of paper containing rules, procedures, guides, and so forth. It became clear that this was an impossible situation for good governance. The board implied acceptable actions by capturing only the unacceptable as limitations, this translated into only two pages of policy. The new policies were easy to read and could be understood immediately. Under these new policies, the organization flourished and became empowered; the emphasis now is on growth and creativity for effectively advancing toward the vision and ENDs.

Positive Benefits of Limitations

The results of limitations policy can be very positive. Limitations are helpful to subordinate groups because the groups are free to determine the hows within the boundaries. If desired hows are within the boundaries, the groups can proceed with their programming. The limitations can help keep activities moving at a fast pace, because subordinate groups and staff know what is not acceptable, and they know all else is.

Limitations policy can be a powerful help to boards and council organizations. The *Chillicothe Bulletin* reported:

The City Council took the following action at its Mar. 14 meeting:

- Approved recommendation from the Planning and Zoning Committee requiring a site plan for the proposed miniature golf course next to the Craft Mall.
- Granted applications submitted for water and sewer connections at 708 and 720 Taylor Drive.
- Instructed the police chief to turn over outdated ballistic vests to the County Sheriff for disposal.
- Approved an expenditure not to exceed $500 for the purchase of three cat traps and two dog traps.

Do these actions sound like rubber stamping? Notice how the spirit of the meeting could have been affected if the Planning Committee, the Water and Sewer Committee, the Police Department, and the dog catcher had been *empowered* by having a good relationship description and a few well-placed limitations.

Limitation Language

Here, again, is the example limitation policy that was offered earlier: "No portion of the organization, whether member or staff, shall cause or allow any practice, activity, or decision that is imprudent, illegal, unethical, or detracts from the purpose of the organization." The broad and general language used may be enforceable by expulsion from membership or termination as an employee.

Limitations for Subordinate Groups

Like relationship policies, the limitations policy category may be divided into two parts: limitations for subordinate groups and limitations for the chief staff officer (staff).

Examples of limitations statements pertinent to subordinate groups may include the following:

- Members may not arbitrarily exclude qualified candidates for membership or operate secretively.

- Members may not accept financial or other goods or benefits that might influence their actions or decisions.
- Members should not endorse special products, patents, processes, individuals, or ideas, except as authorized by the board.
- Members may not speak on behalf of or in a way reserved for the board.

Limitations for Staff

Although staff limitations are similar to those of subordinate groups, staff limitations apply to slightly different circumstances. Some example statements pertinent to the chief staff officer are as follows:

- Foundation funds may not be commingled with operating finances, and assets may not be placed at unprotected risk.
- Staff may not accept financial or other goods or benefits that might influence their actions or decisions.
- Staff may not disburse funds to reimburse members for their travel costs.

Limitations Policy Is a Powerful Concept

Limitations policy is a powerful concept. As an example, one organization had an opportunity to acquire a sizable major resource from a sister organization. Only a brief window of time existed to make the decision. First, the opportunity was directly in concert with the organizational vision. Second, it was judged sound business by the Finance Committee. Third, the responsible subordinate group and staff personnel were convinced of the practicality and desirability of the acquisition, and they were enthusiastic about the opportunity as a powerful means toward the vision. Fourth, positive action was judged by all to be acceptable within the respective boundaries established by the board. So, the subordinate group, in a teaming environment, efficiently and wisely made the decision to proceed with the deal and make the purchase. It would have taken longer to reach a decision if the board were involved—even a rubber-stamp-type decision. Thus, involving the board could have jeopardized the opportunity. This example of implemented empowerment is played over and over at all levels of successful organizations of the future.

Limitations policy is a powerful concept to help build an effective board. Limitations offer only the boundaries of which means are defined as acceptable and then all other activities within those boundaries are acceptable. Progress doesn't require board approval because the effective board already has done its work. In the acquisition example, a large amount of capital was involved. Although the board later supported the process and the decision, the deal was significant enough that the board decided to amend its limitations, stipulating a financial ceiling to ensure the board is involved in very large deals, especially where timing is of less relevance.

An organization operating with a stated limitations policy can flourish because of the established environment of empowerment. Successful organizations of the future will operate without the ball-and-chain of routinely required board approval. Effective boards of the future will predefine vision and direction and predefine limitations for empowered operations. Successful organizations of the future will use these principles to quickly react to change and be more resourceful for creating their future.

Chapter 7

Governance Model Overview

The governance model is a leadership tool that describes all needed facets of organizing vital board policy for progress. It provides answers to fundamental leadership issues of vision, values, authority, and roles. It breaks down all the otherwise complicated aspects of governance into simplified expressions of values divided into four policy segments of ENDs, governance process, relationships, and limitations. As a brief review of the previous four chapters, the four policy segments can be summarized with the following :

- **ENDs (Vision)**—The vision segment describes what good, for whom, and at what cost. ENDs are used for further definition and clarification of the vision.
- **Governance Process**—The governance process segment defines and establishes the governing processes (such as the governing model) expected to be used. This segment shows the desired style of operations and the typical characteristics expected (such as to operate with consensus, trust, respect, and teamwork). It describes the roles and responsibilities of the officers in charge and highlights job products of the board itself.
- **Relationships**—The relationships segment deals with the passing of power and appraisal of its use. It shows all internal and external relationship definitions. This segment establishes all subordinate groups with structure and specified composition, scope/authority, and expected job products. It clarifies delegation and states that all subordinate groups

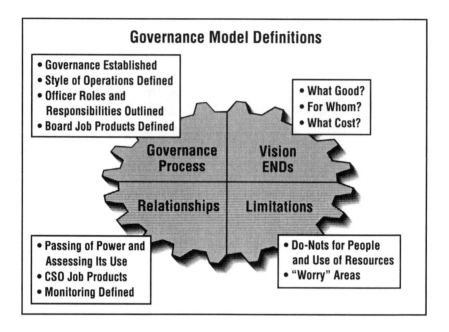

and staff are accountable to the board. It shows the job products of the chief staff officer. It also shows definition policy for the designated monitoring function of the board, including a matrix listing of selected specified measures and the planned frequency of reporting to the board. It can include a policy about external relationships and general expectations for cooperative efforts with those outside.

- **Limitations**—The limitations segment shows the do nots for people and the use of resources including "worry areas" of activity. It establishes boundaries for what is acceptable performance and behavior. This segment actually creates and gives rationale for empowerment. Instead of stating what means are to be used to accomplish the vision of the organization, the limitations permit any and all, large or small, current or new, traditional or original, top-level or low-level means-related activity as long as it conforms within the stipulated boundaries.

Documents Hierarchy

Every organization is predicated on a purpose. Sometimes organizations call this their mission. This purpose or mission is the top level of the documents hierarchy. Next are the articles of incorporation and bylaws of the organization. These documents are member owned and contain the purpose, the basics for the existence of the organization, along with the boiler plate information that is required by the federal government for an organization to exist as an independent organized association entity. These required documents usually are filled with difficult-to-understand legalese-type language. They are unwieldy to change and generally are not conducive as leadership documents for a progressive and effective organization.

The effective board will develop board-owned documents of governance policy that can serve to lead, guide, and manage the organization. These policies include the vision and ENDs policies and the means policies, including governance, relationships, and limitations policies. With the benefit of these board-owned policy

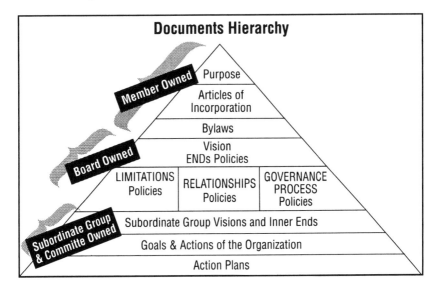

Documents Hierarchy

Member Owned

Purpose
Articles of Incorporation
Bylaws

Board Owned

Vision ENDs Policies
LIMITATIONS Policies | RELATIONSHIPS Policies | GOVERNANCE PROCESS Policies

Subordinate Group & Committe Owned

Subordinate Group Visions and Inner Ends
Goals & Actions of the Organization
Action Plans

documents, the breadth of the organization, including the member subordinate groups and committees and staff, can create inner layers of policy for meeting their particular needs. Additionally, the supportive goals and action plans can now be created that ensure progress toward the vision, which is naturally focused within the overall purpose of being for the organization. This pyramid of documents is fundamental to the successful and effective organization.

Applies to Large and Small Organizations

The governance model can offer new and creative insight to overall leadership of an organization. Application of the governance model also can give transforming powers. Its use can transform the complex into the simple, the ineffective into the effective, and the unauthorized into the empowered in a relatively short period of time. The governance model has a broad range of applications and can be applied successfully to organizations both large and small.

The examples included in this book are intended to give help for building an effective organization—whether large or small. The governance model has much to offer organizations of varying size and constituency. It has intrinsic, positive, and far-reaching application attributes to help a board of directors effectively lead and guide entire organizations of any size. It can be applied to any situation large or small, wherever the authority and resolve resides to define and implement governance. This broad range of application capability unveils the unique power of the governance model to fit all circumstances.

There are many kinds, styles, and classifications of boards. There generally are three major types of boards: corporate, foundation, and association. Although this book focuses on association boards, many of the principles described herein are applicable to all boards.

Within the for-profit world of business, it is common for corporations to have councils, boards, business units, and special groupings of leaders to govern some aspect of the organization, such as a business unit council, research and development review board, quality council, and so forth. These all perform like boards. They do not have direct stockholders, so they are not corporate boards, but they do have many stakeholders like association boards. They are seldom in the business of raising funds, so they are not foundation boards, but they do have resources and monitoring metrics like association boards. Many of these internal boards within the for-profit domain could and should operate more like the effective association board.

Chapter 8

Leadership

Leadership—Where It All Starts

Leadership is the vital ingredient for success of an organization. From leadership comes visions, growth, progress, and achievement. Through leadership, internal power is leveraged. This power turns the cogs of policy, people, and provisions (the components of the engineered organizational model) to provide products and services to meet the needs of customers. Leadership is that almost mystical component of society that is so often misunderstood, obscured, ill-defined, misinterpreted, and underappreciated. But, good leadership is fundamental for the success of any organization.

A Brief Background

The word "leadership" is commonly used today. It is on the lips of politicians, scholars, artists, theologians, philosophers, ministers, business people, and organizational officers the world over. Leadership is the subject of studies, speeches, essays, debates, interviews, memoirs, theses, biographies, articles, and books. Yet, even with all the focus on leadership, never in the history of mankind has there ever been more of a need for this special commodity called leadership.

At one time leadership was considered something people were born with—this gave rise to the term "born leader." The theory goes, if you weren't born with it, you'd never have it. Along the lines of this thinking was the conclusion that less than 1 percent of the population could meet the standards and criteria to be a leader. Either you had it or you didn't. This, of course, was very discouraging for most people—the other 99 percent of the population. In this atmosphere, for an organization to survive and achieve success, leaders were recruited from what was believed to be a shallow well of talent, and it was difficult to find those special people who were supposedly born with this unique skill called leadership.

The born leader idea was replaced by the theory that great events made great leaders. It went something like this: Unless you found yourself in the right place at the right time to exercise and expose those special incubating leadership skills, you never could become a leader. This was a daunting definition for most people, because with this view, it would take boundless courage, extreme conditions, and fateful coincidences to ever become a leader. With this "great events make great leaders" thinking, to become a leader, one must experience some overwhelming challenges and be sifted through screens of near super human capability. In this environment, an organization would need a crisis to take place so that a special leader could "appear" and take personal steps to resolve the major catastrophe as proof of leadership. This leader would somehow surface, establish stability, save the organization, and then this special person would thereafter wear the mantle of leader. It would not be possible for any others to achieve it or obtain leadership until another calamity occurred, where another special person was needed to perform and achieve this greatness called leadership.

Next, there was an attitude that leaders were to be developed, and this gave rise to the trained leader. This theory promoted the concept that with proper training, anyone can become *the* leader. The problem with this concept is that it is too limited in scope. It does not allow room for the evidence of natural talents of people and also implies there can be only as many leaders as there are people trained to be leaders. Training budgets will permit training of only so many, and after all, only a few can be leaders anyway.

The problem with all these definitions of leadership is that they focus on the notion that leadership is exhibited as the skill and a personal quality of an individual. A broader definition suggests that leadership occurs anytime someone influences the behavior of another. Although there are literally hundreds of definitions of leadership, a better definition that is helpful to organizations and their development for the future provides a link between the matters of process and leadership. This definition begins with the statement: *Leadership is a dynamic process....*

Leadership is a dynamic process. Organizations with an eye toward the future need members and staff who are capable of performing with systems and process leadership. This kind of leadership performs without a focus on personal leadership as a quality of an individual; it builds on the strengths of everyone. Process leadership is predicated on the high value and worth of all people. This form of leadership assumes that every team member has special experiences, skills, knowledge, duties, strengths, and a measure of innate desire to perform at his or her best. In these circumstances, uninhibited process leadership naturally swells forth from the teaming environment to produce new and creative solutions of quality leadership to resolve the problems at hand. In this culture, everyone can and is expected to move beyond the ordinary to become extraordinary contributors. This means average people expect to achieve above average, synergistic results over other cultures. Peer pressure is a great contributor to this motivation. Everyone learns to expect the best.

Leadership is a dynamic process, used by the group. This means that the group uses process leadership to rally the best thinking of the team to determine suitable and timely solutions. All aspects of inherent, but sometimes hidden or unperceived personal leadership, are extraordinarily applied with teamwork through the problem-solving process.

Leadership is a dynamic process, used by the group, to produce change. It is through leadership that change is determined, fostered, and applied. Some people resist change, but leadership creates change. In the future, people who are successful will be part of the leadership process teams that are not afraid of change but are creators of change for meeting timely expectations.

Leadership is a dynamic process, used by the group, to produce change, toward the vision. Progress toward the vision is the main reason for, and measure of, success of an activity. It is important that change, which comes from the empowered organization, is created for the express purpose of making progress toward the vision. As people are linked through effective communication channels to the effective board of directors, everyone will have a greater awareness of the vision and direction for the organization. This will pay big dividends because every member of a team, committee, or subordinate group that is working to meet customer expectations, can feel empowered to surface his or her special leadership contribution toward the vision when it is timely.

Leaders Versus Managers

Leaders and managers represent different roles for people to perform. Although some intermingle the terms, it is useful to distinguish between the roles of leaders and managers. Leaders and managers see an organization from two distinctly different points of view, as the following illustrates:

Manager	**Leader**
Focuses on management by objectives	Establishes vectored vision
Values information, understanding, and control functions	Values new technology that opens doors for causing change toward the vision
Spends time planning and budgeting	Spends time setting and communicating a global agenda
Sees people in the organization as staff to accomplish objectives	Sees people as team contributors of ideas for accomplishing missions toward the vision
Has employees	Has followers
Provides controls to staff through commands and telling communications	Empowers and provides motivation and inspiration to encourage people
Expects documentation and reports	Expects celebration of accomplishments
Is good at problem solving and produces order and predictability	Creates problems and produces change with flexibility

Manager	**Leader**
Performs detailed analysis and monitoring	Is intuitive; does broad-based monitoring
Depends on knowledge for detailed monitoring and problem solving	Depends on imagination and creative thinking to lead in the desired direction
Tends to judge and be judged against doing things right	Tends to urge toward doing the right things
Focuses on internal issues	Looks externally beyond the current organization
Uses the left brain, is more analytical and logical, asks how and when things are done	Uses the right brain, uses intuition and emotions, asks what and why questions
Tends to focus on the short term	Tends to focus on the long term
Values training as an essential factor of development	Values education as an essential component of growth
Consciously focuses on low-risk solutions	Accepts some vulnerability and associated risk

Need Both Managers and Leaders

In successful organizations of the future, there is a need for both manager and leader roles. Some would describe the comparison list of attitudes as opposites, 180 degrees apart, each pulling against the other in a tug of war.

A more useful analogy is shown by placing these differences at 90 degrees of each other on an X and Y grid. There is a strong case for describing these attitudes as not opposing, but as complementary and synergistic in nature and both valuable for organizations. For example, the abbreviated list of leader characteristics includes the following: is a visionary for the long-term future, uses imagination to cause change, and delights in flexibility but is vulnerable to short-term results. The abbreviated list of manager characteristics includes the following: is a control expert for the short-term future, uses knowledge to manage for order and predictability, but is averse to risk. As these abbreviated lists indicate, both manager and leader characteristics are necessary to ensure success.

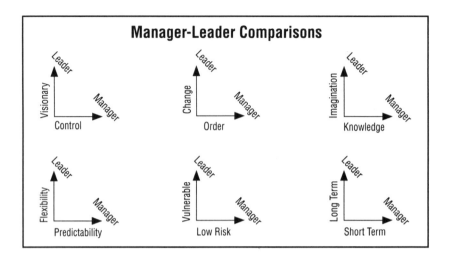

Be a Fourth-Quadrant Organization

Visualizing these characteristics on a grid helps to describe the characteristics of an individual organization by analyzing the relative dominance of each of these manager and leader traits—remembering that each is neither good nor bad, just different. Dominance or balance of manager or leader strengths does, however, make a difference and can yield good or bad situations for an organization.

By plotting on the X and Y coordinates, management versus leadership, it is possible to describe the outwardly visible behaviors and characteristics present within an organization. It is useful to describe these characteristics in terms of four quadrants: Quadrant 1 (Q1) is weak management and weak leadership, quadrant 2 (Q2) is strong management and weak leadership, quadrant 3 (Q3) is weak management and strong leadership, and quadrant 4 (Q4) is strong management and strong leadership.

An organization where both management and leadership are weak (Q1) exhibits characteristics of special interests with an internal focus, while being bogged down in vast detail. A board meeting in this environment usually includes numerous agenda items, detailed in nature, driven from sources internal to the organization. In this atmosphere, the board feels frustrated at the lack of progress and an overall apprehension that it is just too difficult to make a difference. Individually, members of the board may be strong leaders and/or managers, but the organization as a whole exhibits Q1-type thinking with bogged down attitudes. This kind of organization cannot be expected to last very long.

An organization that exhibits strong management and weak leadership (Q2) is very focused on short-term results, even though it may have great long-term managerial projections. It forces control, order, and predictability. There is a strong emphasis on getting the knowledge for decision making and problem solving, but all with a relatively short-term view of the future. Only very low-risk thinking occurs, so creative visions for the future are not considered. With strong management and weak leadership, a stable organization has the potential to survive for an extended time by sustaining progress from the momentum of the past. The future, however, promises a culture of increasingly rapid change. It will be more and more difficult for this type of organization to survive.

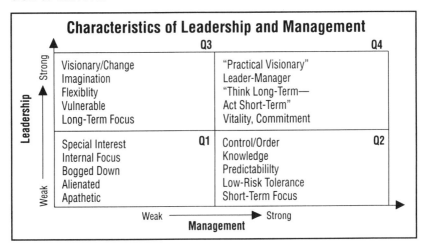

An organization that exhibits weak management and strong leadership (Q3) is focused intensely on the long-term vision and direction for the organization. There is high interest in causing change by using imagination and stretch-type thinking. Flexibility dominates in all aspects of leading the organization, and the short-term managing is weak and not getting proper attention. Because of all the long-term focus, the organization is vulnerable and may not stay solvent and ever achieve the long-term vision. Even in a culture of rapidly increasing change, with weak management, it will be difficult for this type of organization to survive to make much progress toward even the greatest and most noble long-range vision.

An organization that exhibits strong management and strong leadership can be called a fourth-quadrant organization. A fourth-quadrant organization includes people who are practical visionaries. This organization is able to perform with leadership, but also contains a balance of the skills of management. The leader-manager organization is one that can think in the long term, but act in the short term. Fourth-quadrant organizations are the only type of organization that can hope for a bright future. All others are at very high risk of failure.

Growth Journey to Fourth-Quadrant Success

Some organizations that exhibit the characteristics of quadrant one or two should consider possibilities of how to move beyond the current situation. It is possible to achieve fourth-quadrant success if there is resolve and determination to strengthen leadership. Often, organizations will begin with a strong leadership environment but with not enough management (Q3). A meaningful progression shows a march through all four of the quadrants over a period of time. The rate of progress will depend on commitment, timing, use of outside resources, and other factors, but progress through these quadrants is necessary if there is to be sustained hope for the future. This movement through the quadrants toward success may be called the growth journey.

For example, an organization could begin in quadrant two with strong management and weak leadership. This organization came with strong momentum from the past, but over time and with the complexities of change, the management has weakened, things have become bogged down, and the organization moves to quadrant one.

At this point, the board of directors realizes that something must be done. Morale is low, satisfaction is down and low, and results are less than desired. Evidence of warfare within the executive ranks is commonplace, and the board is always inward looking. Now a catalyst appears; the board's effectiveness totally bottoms out, and it is recognized that something must be done. This drives a determination and a commitment to change—a commitment to explore good governance and to get on the right track. The board exercises leadership and is determined to establish a vision; it moves to quadrant three.

This move is refreshing but requires dedication and hard work. The board tackles this challenge and works quickly, knowing the risk of delay. The future vitality of the organization still is very much at risk at this place in the cycle, but the board wisely takes time to establish vision and the beginnings of good governance while expecting the solvent part of subordinate groups and staff to hold things together for the short term. As the board regroups, the governance model is implemented and the beginnings of the thinking as shown in the engineered organizational model are evident. With continued effort, progressive policies, total quality, and monitoring measures are implemented, and the board moves to quadrant four.

The models are implemented throughout the organization, and a new culture of empowerment is established. The board now is demonstrating effectiveness, with visibility and purpose. The board leads, guides, and directs the whole organization onward. This fourth-quadrant thinking grows and flourishes and becomes the established culture for calculated, expected, and inevitable long-term success.

Fourth-Quadrant Attitudes

There are special differences between managers and leaders, but the contributions of each are valuable. Too often people become categorized as a manager or leader based on their natural thinking patterns. There is evidence, however, that depending on the nature of the situation, people can switch hats of manager or leader. These role reversals provide a healthy progressive environment toward becoming fourth-quadrant thinkers.

An effective board will have members who, as a composite, yield fourth-quadrant thinking with fourth-quadrant attitudes. They will embody the vision for the whole organization and make it real to all related people. They will set high expectations and monitor the progress as change is caused. They will model the challenge of leadership and always be collecting and demonstrating application of innovative ideas to meet the needs of customers. They will encourage, recognize, and reward risk taking to ensure progress toward the vision because they realize it was actually less risk to take some risk to establish vision and governance with the promise of progress rather than take no risk and remain stagnant—and fail.

This fourth-quadrant thinking provides leverage to the cogs of policy, people, and provisions. It is this form of leadership that discloses the effective board of directors and makes vivid the effective total organization.

Chapter 9

Board and Chief Staff Officer Relationships

Board/Staff Relationship—A Critical Success Factor

The relationship between the board of directors and the chief staff officer probably is the most critical human factor that determines progress and the rate of success of any organization. The relationship can vary on a scale from "very friendly and effective" to "cold and adversarial." The degree of trust and honesty in this relationship will dictate the position on the relationship scale. It also is accepted that the relationship between the board chairperson and the chief staff officer will establish the model for member and staff relationships throughout the organization. These relationships, in effect, set the operational tone for the entire organization and are critical in establishing the working atmosphere for the future.

The alliance between the board and the chief staff officer will affect progress directly and ultimately determines how well the organization achieves its goals. If there is too much discord, progress will be slower than desired, problems will go unresolved, and many special opportunities will go unanswered or unnoticed. However, if the alliance is strong, positive signals will be sent to the membership and staff as a whole. In this atmosphere, an organization can flourish and achieve the successes that will make people proud to be a part of the organization. The stronger the relationship and the greater the alignment of the partners, the greater the progress and success potential.

A Partnership and Team Relationship

Board and staff relationships can be described best as a team or partnership, and it is not so much a matter of individual strength. Some would argue that a weak staff gives rise to a strong board or a weak board gives rise to a strong staff—neither of which is ideal. A powerful organization can have a strong board and at the same time have a strong chief staff officer and staff. Strong partners, with a strong relationship of trust and honesty aligned toward the same vision, is the ideal. The stronger the partners, the greater the progress potential.

Drawbacks in Staff-Driven Organizations

The modern trend is toward greater professionalism in the ranks of staff. This has given rise to stronger staff and a tendency toward more staff-driven organizations. Boards of staff-driven organizations easily can become involved in rubber-stamping activities, which support strong staff. These boards exhibit less involvement and, therefore, lack commitment in decision making. Often, board members will, consciously or not, sit back and let staff do all the work, including board work. In this case, the board will have limited feelings of satisfaction and, ironically, a lower appreciation of staff efforts than staff think they deserve. Staff will be continually and sometimes unconsciously on guard to defend their actions. They may even have misunderstood fears that the board may "wake up" some day and not be happy any more. For many reasons, this staff-driven situation is loaded with pitfalls.

Drawbacks in Member-Driven Organizations

The other end of the continuum is the member-driven organization. In this case, member officers are at the root of making major decisions, broad decisions, detailed decisions, even those operational decisions normally delegated to the chief staff officer and staff. Although member involvement and commitment is high, time delays in decision making become a typical and increasingly serious problem. This gives rise to less-than-expected progress for the organization, and morale decreases on all fronts.

Although some board members love to gain this power, they do so to derive several benefits. For example, certain board members may achieve prized personal specialized goals because they can make things happen and few others can block these moves. They may rally the help of key executives and employees then "go for it" to achieve their own personal desires. They often are treated well by others and lauded with compliments. They may even come to see their power as a valued end in itself and as a natural part of their role as board members. They develop an attachment to this power and try to preserve it at all costs. Staff executives, meanwhile, become operating zombies, powerless to manage priorities to meet member needs. All this is happening while others, including peer board members, are dominated, underutilized, ineffective, and even bored.

Market-Directed Organizations—The Best Balance

According to Glenn Tecker and Marybeth Fidler, in *Successful Association Leadership,* successful organizations of the future will move toward the market-directed or knowledge-based profile. Tecker says, "In this organizational portrait, who makes the decision (whether staff or member) is not nearly as important as the quality of information on which the decisions are made. A rational common data base must be developed and maintained to guide decisions about member wants, needs, and preferences.... It allows decision making to occur at the point in the organization where the decision can best be made, as defined by the need rather than by hierarchy or territory."

Organizations that are willing to move beyond traditional roles can establish new teaming relationships for the greater good of the organization. This kind of thinking will allow and maximize the involvement, knowledge, commitment, and expertise of all

concerned. Everyone wins in this approach; all stakeholders—
present and future—benefit from knowledge-based thinking.
Leaders who are willing to and interested in learning this approach will be rewarded with fulfillment and success. This approach provides a focus on "who are the stakeholders?" and "what
do the stakeholders want?" Through this kind of thinking, organizations can develop a superior approach to meeting needs and
an advanced process of working together to accomplish the organi
zation's vision.

Success in Relationships

Against this backdrop of optimizing the balance of power for the
organization, there are four key steps to finding success in mem-
ber/staff relationships. They start with recruiting the chief staff officer. Many qualities need to be exercised in the daily routine of
performing the duties of this position. Successful recruiting begins with determining the qualities expected for the job at hand.
Next, the board must define the overall expectations of the job.
These expectations should be written as job products and defined
in relationships policy in the governance model. It is important
that no surprises about job expectations show up later. Additionally, each year, specific goals should be identified and communicated between the chief staff officer and board. Every board
should establish an annual mechanism for performance evaluation. The fourth step is to communicate and gain prior commitment by all (particularly at the board and executive level) to
progress toward greater accomplishments. Because of the relative
importance of these four elements in the success of board/staff
relationships, each one is now described in more detail.

1. Recruit a Good Chief Staff Officer

The success of any board/staff relationship begins with hiring and
retaining the most qualified and capable individual for the job.
Remember, there are two independent elements for this board/

staff success—strength and alignment. The board should not be afraid to hire a top candidate for the job. A strong chief staff officer, when aligned with a strong board, is the best way to ensure future success. This mutual strength and alignment can foster complementary actions and yield outstanding synergistic results.

Core competencies need to be identified by the board, because they are fundamental to selecting the best candidate. The list of competencies will vary from organization to organization, depending on many factors. Some core competencies include experience and knowledge in working with a board, operations management, financial planning, team-building skills, public relations, communications, and speaking skills. In the interview process, questions should solicit feedback on experiences in the identified core competencies. Later, these can be evaluated by the group to systematically analyze the relative strengths of each candidate in each of these areas.

It is the board's job product to hire the chief staff officer. A subteam or subcommittee of the board can be established to perform some of the up-front search duties of the recruitment process, but the board needs to have ultimate control. The full board should be the decision-making body. A subteam may do some prescreening, based on established board desires, to narrow down the selection to the top two or three candidates for the position, but the board never should delegate the job of hiring the chief staff officer.

Take a Long View. Although there is no easy way to accomplish this big task, the board should get organized for what can be an exciting and rewarding experience. The board needs to establish the job products and expectations for the position—the long view. These should be well established and written in board policy in the relationships and limitations portion of the policy manual. No surprises are acceptable in this area of job expectations.

Take a Short View. In addition to the long view, the board also should take the short view. It is appropriate to draft the desired goals for the expected accomplishments of the first year. What are the short-term expectations of the board? This can be negotiated later, as necessary, but early documentation by the board allows the board to determine what is important and needed at this point in time for the organization. This combination of taking the long and short view will optimize success for both the board and the candidate.

Next, the board should perform an honest analysis of the current status of the organization. This should include financial and personnel factors, as well as public relations and board attitudes. These also should be documented in such a way as to help in honest two-way communication with the candidate.

The board should make visible the annual performance evaluation process. This process should be clear throughout the selection process, otherwise it may foster problems for the board and the candidate after the first year.

Critical Work of the Board—Hiring the Chief Staff Officer. Selecting a chief staff officer is one of the most important decisions a board can make. This single decision can make or break the organization. The board must step up to this responsibility with professionalism and do the best job possible.

One principle of human nature to keep in mind is that a person likely will do more of what he or she has done in the past. A person's track record provides a strong indication of what he or she is likely to do in the future. Although impressive resumes can be helpful, board members should look beyond the words and "fluff" and quickly focus on the results, because, ultimately, it is actual performance that matters.

One approach to selecting the best candidate is the STAR (Situation, Task, Action, and Result) system of targeted selection. This system of targeted selection was developed by Development Dimensions International, Pittsburgh, Pennsylvania. The STAR system is predicated on the belief that people will do in the future more of what they have demonstrated in the past, and it is through effective interviewing processes that past dimensions of the talents, skills, and job characteristics can be evaluated and judged in comparison with future job requirements.

When interviewing and evaluating candidates, it is wise to document past special events and happenings that demonstrate the behaviors and skills sought. If these traits cannot be found in the first candidate, then keep looking. Effective interviewing involves identifying examples that do the following:

- Situation—Show the candidate in some situation
- Task—Identify what task was important or needed to make improvements
- Action—Identify what actions the candidate actually performed
- Results—Describe the results of those actions (results being either good or not so good)

Analyzing the STARs for each candidate helps to highlight the strongest candidate with the strongest desired behaviors, skills, and aptitudes. Interview questions should be structured to determine STARs, particularly in the areas of needed and desired core competencies.

Tips for Effective Interviews. The following tips for effective interviews include ideas that can help persons become better interviewers and, therefore, able to make more accurate appraisals of candidates.

1. Be prepared. Have the job description. Know the key requirements. Have a copy of the resume. Have pertinent questions ready.
2. Have several people involved in the interview process. The finalist should spend some time before the full board.
3. Candidates should have information about the job, the organization, and the local community before interviews.
4. Interviews should be conducted in quiet, confidential settings. Have at least one interview conducted over a meal or in social setting.
5. Interviews should be more like discussions with a back-and-forth exchange of ideas, but the candidate should do most of the talking.

6. Ask open-ended questions—questions that cannot be answered with a simple yes or no. Look for the "why" of behavior and "chemistry."

7. A significant part of the interview should concern past behavior. Focus questions on what, why, how, when, where, and who issues.

8. Avoid questions about a person's sex, age, race, religion, or national background. Look for STARs.

9. Screen candidates and applicants over the telephone before inviting anyone in for a personal interview.

10. Don't ignore getting the spouse involved before an offer is extended. Is a move acceptable to the family?

11. Investigate several candidates at first, then narrow down the list to the most promising candidate for a longer, more intensive interview.

12. Take notes during the interview so that you don't forget key points. After the interview, record all the STARs and impressions.

13. After each interview, describe what will happen next, when applicants can expect to hear more. Follow up with a thank you note.

2. Define the Expectations for the Chief Staff Officer

The second of the four key steps to finding success in member/staff relationships is to define the expectations of the job. The board should define the responsibilities and job products of the chief staff officer and document those in the relationships section of the governance policy manual.

Key expectations and accountabilities can be as brief or as detailed as desired and needed by the respective parties (the board or the chief staff officer). Expectations and accountabilities may include the following:

• Ability to achieve ENDs (have competent staff team, implement goals and plans for support, use progression and succession personnel plans, provide timely counsel to all appropriate stakeholders)

- Safety of organizational assets and legal status (provide proper security, police legal abuses, and so forth)
- Accurate and timely information (provide staff input to the board and membership, monitor trends, provide counsel)
- Public relations among appropriate areas (establish and maintain positive perceptions of the organization)
- Communications channel (communicate across the breadth and depth of the organization for the benefit of all)

Whatever the board of directors expects of its chief staff officer should be written down in relationships policy so there is no confusion. The board should set aside as much time as needed to fully define these expectations.

3. Do an Annual Performance Review and Evaluation

Every employee of any organization should receive an annual performance review and evaluation. In the case of the chief staff officer, this sometimes can be confusing, difficult, and awkward if not done properly. The board has one and only one employee, and that person is the chief staff officer. It is the job of the board to administer the annual performance evaluation for that special employee.

There are many ways and means of performing the annual performance evaluation, but occasionally, it is appropriate to take a fresh approach in light of the governance policy model. Because the relationships policy defines the job products for the chief staff officer, the annual performance review should begin there. The key question of the board should be: "How has this employee performed against those job product expectations written in board policy?"

Be Sure the Chief Staff Officer Has Communication Time for the Board. One important tool is the set of annual goals crafted by the chief staff officer, concurred by the president, copied to the board, and communicated frequently with ongoing results. The chief staff officer should provide status reports and updates as part of regular board meeting agendas. When board agendas are assembled, the chief staff officer, and occasionally appropriate direct reports, should have time on board agendas to provide information on trends and progress. This helps to appraise the board of the performance progress of its employee. Sometimes board members will advocate no time on the agenda for staff input. This can be a problem, because not making information available indicates either poor performance or poor communication. If poor staff performance is the problem, then board agenda time is needed to correct deficiencies. If communication is the problem and information is not available because no time is allocated, then the board is not getting its full and fair value from its employee and the board is not operating from a knowledge-based environment. In either case, the board needs and deserves some custodial, staff communication on virtually every agenda.

Some key regular executive communication is necessary to build and maintain trust, honesty, and a good working relationship at the executive levels of the organization. It may be appropriate to define what is "some" communication. Monitoring organizational performance, as a general rule, should be kept to a minimum of board time for efficiency purposes. But at virtually every board meeting there should be enough (not extended) exposure of the chief staff officer or key staff direct report(s) for the board to make judgments as to the level of performance progress on a personal and corporate basis. This ensures no surprises at the end of the year, when the formal performance evaluation is done.

Document the Annual Performance Review Process. As the year unfolds and it comes time to conduct the annual performance review, the board should have a documented plan for handling the process professionally. This process begins with the custodial input of the goals for the coming year from the chief staff officer. The president, as the single representative of the employer (the board), should meet with the board's employee (the chief staff officer) to finalize the list of goals. These goals, at a minimum, should be sent to the compensation committee or special annual performance review subteam of the board charged with the chief staff officer annual evaluation and even to the full board, perhaps in the meeting minutes as part of the chief staff officer custodial report. Communication early in the year can have profound benefits as the year unfolds and results start to be compared against the stated goals for the year. If the board has expectations other than those stated in the goals, then early clarification is desirable and still possible at this time.

Modern team-type thinking suggests that more input is better for this annual performance review process. More and more organizations are adopting a 360-degree method of input. This includes input from the board (the boss), input from direct reports of the chief staff officer (the executive-level staff), direct input from the employee (the chief staff officer), and input from any other appropriate peers inside or outside the organization. Using all these inputs can improve the annual performance review process and make the president's job of compiling the initial draft of the annual performance appraisal more straight forward. The board needs to determine and document whether it wants to delegate the responsibility to a subteam of the board, a compensation committee, or some other group, or retain this as personal job of the full board. Once this has been decided, the process should be documented in job product expectations. In any case, it should be made clear from board relationships policy that an annual performance evaluation will be performed and it is synonymous with monitoring organizational performance against applicable board policies.

4. Communicate and Gain Commitment

The fourth key step to finding success in member/staff relationships is to communicate fully. Effective communication helps gain compatible commitment for progress toward the vision and ENDs of the organization. Some board members become weary of developing policy. Some even try to put this communication method into the negative category of "wordsmithing." Effective communication, however, is in no way wordsmithing as long as the board agrees the word choices are good enough and the board is willing to accept any reasonable interpretation. It is important that a board spend sufficient time in developing documented board policy to lead and guide the organization. Others can create publications and verbally communicate the message, but it is up to the board to clarify and document the basis for subsequent communication. Effective communication begins in the board room.

One of the typical job products of the board of directors is to be a link and communicator among leaders. One of the job products of the chief staff officer may be public relations. This also means communication. Effective communication on the part of the board and chief staff officer serves as a model for the organization as a whole. Effective communication also allows various important issues to be made visible to the breadth of the organization. Effective communication at the board and chief staff officer level models organization values that can be leveraged throughout. Because effective intraorganizational communication at the highest levels of the organization is inherently perceived, observed, and recognized by others at all positions of the organization, this automatically becomes the paradigm for others to follow. This is how a good culture of communication is fostered.

Chapter 10

Training and Orientation

Why Train?

John was elected to be a new board member. He went to his first board meeting with enthusiasm and interest but he felt a little anxious about what contribution he would make. At this first meeting, the agenda was filled with numerous, detailed, complex, and seemingly important issues. He came into the meeting open minded, unbiased, and ready to make his contribution, but uncertain as to his expected role. There had been no training or orientation for the board members, so he was getting on-the-job training as the meeting unfolded. As each issue was raised, there was always a senior, self-assured member of the board who seemed greatly informed and intimately interested in every subject.

Because of the knowledge and determination of that person, few of the other board members were given any real opportunity to speak up. John did not feel comfortable contributing to the discussion. So John went home without ever experiencing an unthreatening opportunity to make a contribution—other than to raise his hand to vote with the group at the obvious time. The atmosphere was intimidating. He was glad he had not been put on the spot to speak—he had just listened throughout the entire meeting and did not say a word.

New board members often remain silent or speak up only to follow group expectations. Sometimes they are intimidated by either the meeting aura and format or more experienced and knowledgeable peers. Too often, this story is repeated again and again, particularly for incoming board members. Lack of participation is a lose/lose condition—a waste of the talents, potential, and resources available to the organization and loss of the personal rewards and self-satisfaction that could be gained by new board members.

How can new board members be part of a win/win situation for both the organization and themselves? The answer is twofold: governance and training.

First an effective system of governance, such as one based on the governance model, needs to be implemented to define roles, build a structure and pattern for meetings and agendas, determine expectations for board members, and instill sound meeting mechanics. Effective governance provides a process for establishing the vision and policy while marking progress toward the future that even the newest board member can understand. Second, training and orientating incoming board members is essential.

The Purpose of Training and Orientation

There are many reasons for training and orientating incoming board members. Well-planned and well-executed training and orientation programs help shape board member expectations and overcome lack of understanding. In addition, they can create the teaming paradigm and guard against early inappropriate behavior.

Training and orientation will help incoming board members be aware of pertinent information about the organization and gain early knowledge and insights of current vision, goals, programs, products, and services. Training and orientation also should be provided to show what the governance system is, how it works, the role the board member is expected to perform, and how his or her involvement and personal participation is valuable to the organization.

The key factors for having trained and oriented, top-performing, and effective new board members involve several phases. The process begins with a progressive definition of the term of office, identification of realistic qualifications and expectations of the job, a good recruiting process, early scheduled orientation and training before the first board meeting, vacancies that are quickly filled, and organized ongoing governance refreshers.

Term-of-Office Factors

The terms of office for the board of directors vary for different organizations, but terms can affect the board's effectiveness and dictate the needs for training and orientation. Usually, the terms of office are defined in the bylaws, which describe not only the length of the term of office but the maximum length of service and limits to reelection intervals and number of terms. A style of overlapping terms is a progressive term-of-office process in common practice for boards today. This method calls for the annual election of, say, one-third of the board members for a three-year term.

This method of overlapping terms of office (staggered terms) provides opportunities for a strong and effective board for two reasons. First, in this example, one-third of the board would be new each year, which ensures an influx of new board members to keep the board fresh. Long-time board members sometimes tend to become complacent, indifferent, and passive in their thinking; this can grow to become a cancerous detriment in this fast-moving and rapidly changing world. Second, using this system of overlapping terms, each year the board would retain two-thirds of the previous year's members, which preserves continuity. Both reasons contribute to the strength and vitality of an effective board.

When using overlapping or staggered terms for board members, it is important not to be lulled into thinking that board orientation and training is not required. With one-third of the board new each year (and this is a significantly high percentage) a new team exists. Although it can be argued that two-thirds of the board still is experienced, it can be argued further that because one-third of the board is new, a whole new board now exists. It is important to recognize that a team must be built and continually rebuilt with *all* the members, not just the new members. Even when a single new board member is added, a totally new board is formed, and training again becomes very important.

Meeting Expectations Requires Skills and Training

The next key factor for having effective board members lies in having realistic qualifications and expectations for new board members. New board members should embody known skills that can contribute to the success of the organization. These skills, when applied with appropriate orientation and training, can be especially valuable for growth by using and applying tools such as the governance model. The organization can benefit in many ways from the involvement of new board members. In turn, new board members can benefit greatly from the organization, by quickly gaining a special sense of reward and worth as their personal participation becomes self-evident.

Desirable board members are committed and have time, resources, knowledge, contacts, management skills, and leadership abilities to contribute to their roles on the board. Questions to consider when evaluating potential board members include the following:

- Could this person bring important, fresh, and timely insights to the board?
- What is the board's diversity quotient currently, and is it relevant that this person be a minority or female?
- Does this person represent the membership segment that gives the best balance of the board at this time?
- Is this person experienced? Does he or she have leadership qualities that could help strengthen the board in needed areas now?
- Is this person a senior-level executive? Does he or she have the prestige and esteem that could be important to the organization currently?

- Does this person have contacts in important places that could be valuable and significant for opening doors for the progress of the organizational vision, or does this person have personal wealth and make significant contributions to the organization as an indication that he or she really cares about the causes of the organization?
- Is this person highly involved in the organization? (This involvement may be an indication of interest, knowledge, and commitment.)
- Is the geographical location of this person a factor that could be beneficial (or, on the other hand, a problem) for the future?

One method of evaluation is to list all these criteria on a chart, with the names of each of the potential candidates. Then, the board can rate each person in each of these categories. The values may be defined as 3 for high, 2 for medium, and 1 for low, for each of the current needs of the board. If each of these criteria is of equal weight, the board simply works through the chart for each potential new member. If some criteria are considered much more pertinent than others, then a weighting factor could be applied as appropriate. One board used this weighting factor idea when they were working with this type of matrix process to select a person to fill a board vacancy. In this example, the all-male board gave double weighting to the diversity factor. As it turned out, with all other qualifications of similar strength, a female candidate was in fact elected to the board over several male candidates.

Next, by filling in the values for each, then totaling the columns, a relative strength can be determined. The strongest candidate will have the highest total. Although these factors can be tailored for any respective organization, the purpose of an evaluation method is to provide an unbiased analysis technique (for this point in time against the current needs) for selection of the best candidate for the board.

Evaluation Method for Selecting Board Members				
	Candidates			
	#1	**#2**	**#3**	**#4**
Fresh insights to the Board?				
Minority or female?				
Membership segment balance?				
Experienced in leadership?				
Senior-level executive?				
Has contacts and/or personal wealth?				
Highly involved in the organization?				
Geographical location factor?				
Total				

3 = High Need in Board   2 = Medium Need in Board   1 = Low Need in Board

New Member Recruiting

The next key factor for effective board members is a good recruiting process. Good board members are a must. A good organization can be only as strong as the board leading it. A stable organization needs board members who are mature and able to weather the storms and problems for proactive decision making. A positive view of the future requires an organized view of recruiting for the present.

Many boards are bound by bylaws that stipulate how future new board members are selected and elected. In this case, the current board may have little to say about who is elected, and consequently, the recruiting process often is indirect at best. This highlights the need for a good process to find and obtain the best board members to help build an effective board for the future. Here are some tips to help ensure success.

Have a Process—Usually, the bylaws will include some overview of the nominating and election process for new members of the board of directors. Often, a nominating committee is formed, with selected and specified members serving on this committee. The bylaws likely will contain articles on voting rights and overview procedures for the conduct of elections.

In addition to the bylaws, some detailed rules and procedures should be established and adopted by the board of directors. These procedures are vital to maintain the highest integrity in the mechanics of how the process is handled and how new board members are determined.

Highlight Qualifications and Expectations—To gain the highest quality for incoming new board members, the highest qualifications and expectations need to be visible. An effective board that is integrating good governance throughout the organization will have exposed numerous members and future potential candidates, either directly or indirectly, to this style of governance. So, strong candidates for the board already may have exhibited the ability to think in terms of vision, systems, and processes and may have shown interest in greater understanding of the governance model, along with willingness and commitment to become involved. The names of these people need to find their way into the nomination process.

The President Promotes Awareness All Year—As the president and the chief staff officer travel throughout the year and make contacts within the organization, good future board member candidates naturally will become obvious to them. These people should be encouraged to get to know the election process, establish their network to make visible this goal to become a member of the board, and create an appropriate awareness of this interest and willingness to become involved as a member of the board. It is a better problem to have too many interested individuals than to have not enough candidates.

Early Orientation of Incoming Board Members

The next key factor for having effective board members is early orientation with those who have been elected and are incoming to the board. Usually, there is some time between the announcement of election results and the first board meeting they will be attending. This period before their first board meeting is a good window for early proactive orientation. This orientation can vary from a simple one-on-one meeting with the chief staff officer or the president to more elaborate sessions of introduction with staff and other member leaders. Do whatever best fits your culture, as long as some minimum of basic orientation is completed before the first board meeting.

Have a Plan (Who, When, and Where)—The early orientation needs to be planned. For example, assuming overlapping terms of office, some new board members will be moving onto the board each year. It is a good practice to have the chief staff officer or president perform this initial orientation of the new board member-elect. This orientation meeting should be scheduled to take place several weeks before the first board meeting is to be held. The orientation meeting should be held at a convenient location. At this point, it is not necessary for extensive meetings and personnel introductions because this can be done more effectively later, when new board members are better oriented about their position.

Have Defined Materials (What and Why)—What are the most appropriate things to discuss at this time? The beginnings of the board manual should be assembled by staff and provided to the new board member-elect. This manual should contain the following basic items, at a minimum: the board policy manual (all four segments), bylaws, list of current and incoming board members with addresses and phone numbers, an organization chart, a list of staff, and the last annual report.

The agenda for this meeting should be an overview of this book of reference materials, focusing on two areas of the policy manual: (1) the vision and ENDs and (2) the role of the board. This agenda can lead to an exciting meeting and establish great expectations and interest.

Training Before First Board Meeting

The next key factor for having effective board members is governance training before the first board meeting. Ideally, all incoming board members should be invited as guests to at least one of the board meetings before taking office. As guests, the board member-elect can witness first-hand how the board practices governance. This also can offer valuable early understanding of the current issues at hand.

Have a Plan (When, Where, Who)—Training just before the first board meeting is important. In fact, this can take place on the first day and at the same location of a multiday board meeting, or it can be set up, for example, on the afternoon before the first board meeting. Knowing that the teacher learns the most, it is a good idea to have some current board members involved in training incoming board members rather than using only an outside consultant or the same staff person all the time. This can be a period of team learning because everyone can enter into the process of growing in the knowledge of governance.

Have Appropriate Materials (What)—The main purpose of this type of training is for the incoming board member to be fully aware of the governance model, the governance process, types of policy, and the roles and expectations of the board. This session can follow along an agenda of the following items:

- The governance model overview
- Quiz questions about ENDs versus means
- When to create policy, the role of the board
- Quiz questions on policy types

Governance Quizzes (ENDs versus Means)—The question often asked is, "Is this a means or an ENDs statement?" Appendix B offers examples to help sharpen the skill at responding to this question. The purpose of this exercise is to help review definitions of the governance model for these provided hypothetical scenarios. As answers are given, recognize the answers should be not whether you believe it should be a means or an ENDs, but can you prove it by the governance model and appropriate board policy?

Fill Board Vacancies Quickly

The next key factor for having effective board members is to fill board vacancies quickly. Occasionally, board vacancies will occur. The many reasons for these vacancies range from work-related conflicts to time-related pressures or health-related problems. Rarely will a board member be removed by legal proceedings, but it could occur if the member is unable to faithfully fulfill the duties and responsibilities of the position.

The bylaws or policy should include language for how vacancies are to be filled. Provisions are necessary to fill board vacancies. Some bylaws require a special election by the membership; others establish that the board fill the vacancy itself. Whatever the process used, it is important to have vacancies filled at the earliest opportunity. For a board to be most effective, members should build and have a teaming spirit that comes through productive time, creating results, and celebrating accomplishments. Any later additions of members to the team will require more orientation, and building time, to yield the same characteristics for all board members.

Ongoing Governance Refreshers

An effective board may choose to take opportunities to advance its knowledge of governance by creating and giving quiz questions to the board team as a form of light entertainment with a flair for learning. The materials and the context can be simple. Using the examples offered the appendix may be helpful.

Chapter 11

Teams and Consensus

It Takes a Team to Win

In his book *High Output Management,* Andrew S. Grove, president of Intel, says "it always takes a team to win." This belief is increasingly widespread in today's fast-changing environment. It is true in sports, politics, business, associations, and boards. Teams are critical in any situation where people unite for a common good.

Whenever people come together to work together, they shape a culture. This culture is a complex network of traditions, values, beliefs, and expectations that describes the emotional, social, and psychological foundations on which decisions are made. One of the job products of the board is to document values in the form of expressions of policy (the policy manual) to lead, guide, and direct the organization in a common and consistent manner. Teams are a natural outgrowth of the need to move beyond the autocratic thinking of the past. There is not enough hours in the day for restrictive decision making, so teams are becoming a powerful component of this new culture.

Teams—The Arms and Legs of Empowerment

The use of teams is an idea ready for widespread implementation into organizational culture. Teams are the arms and legs of the empowered organization. Teams are an essential ingredient for success of the future to make required gains in efficiency. However, because teams can have some pitfalls, teams must be implemented effectively.

There are many definitions of teams. According to Jon R. Katzenbach and Douglas K. Smith in *The Wisdom of Teams,* "a team is a small number of people with complementary skills who are committed to a common purpose, performance goals, and approach for which they hold themselves mutually accountable."

Teams have been shown to be beneficial in advancing all aspects of quality, meeting customer needs, improving product and process performance, and implementing more timely responses to problem solving in general. The teaming environment is a culture that moves beyond the past stagnant atmosphere of tightly controlled information that is known only by those in high places. The teaming culture permits the right information to be provided to the right people so the best, timely, and "right" decisions can be made.

Teams are established and authorized to accomplish those desired goals and actions that move an organization toward the vision. Teams can be established to accomplish governance tasks within the board of directors. Teams receive delegated responsibility at the time they are established. That responsibility never should be taken back by the authorizing leadership.

The teaming culture is relatively new and still is advancing. Different expectations can exist from all levels, including the board of directors, staff, and team members. As the team concept permeates the organizational culture, however, the future can yield a hierarchy of teams—teams starting within the board itself to tiers of teams compounding throughout the whole of the organization.

Executive Committee Versus Teams

In the environment of teams, a board of directors may choose to use teams to increase the effectiveness of the board and apply this thinking to the executive committee of the board of directors. There are various opinions about using an executive committee, but at best, using an executive committee is burdened with numerous pitfalls that can greatly diminish the effectiveness of the board.

Some of the pitfalls of using an executive committee are evident. Often, for example, the problems begin with the initial appointments. When those special five or six board members are appointed to the executive committee at the beginning of the year, they commonly are viewed as "super board members" by their peers. Instantly, some degree of disharmony and disunity is created. This situation can emerge subtly—barely showing—or boldly—outwardly dominant. In any case, once an executive committee is appointed, the rest of the board members may feel concerned, uneasy, and even jealous.

Often, an executive committee will entertain agenda items unknown by the full board. Even in the purest spirit of doing useful work between full board meetings, it is difficult to avoid the impression of having agendas hidden from the full board. Trust is difficult to foster with these natural pitfalls built into the existence of an executive committee. Although agenda items may be well within their specified authorization, over time, problems with these agenda items can lead to higher degrees of disharmony and disunity.

Sometimes, an executive committee will perform interim business duties that could be handled later by the full board. It may be argued that if the subject was so important that it needed action before the next board meeting, then this subject is more detailed than is appropriate for board action. Perhaps it should have been a delegated issue. On the other hand, if it really was a governance topic for the board, then handling by the executive committee is insufficient anyway.

It also can be argued that if the board is so busy that some work needs to be farmed out to an executive committee without the benefit of full board action, then this work is more detailed than is needed for exercising good governance within the board. There always is too much work to do. That is why a good board will predefine and prioritize its annual agenda. An effective board will work with unity, strengthened by diversity, to build strong board policies and decisions. Farming out work to be done invisible to the board inherently creates disunity and therefore is risky business.

Subteams of the Board Leverage Involvement

By using subteams, a board can leverage board member involvement in a positive way much more powerfully than by using an
executive committee. The following are some comparisons.

The executive committee is formed early in the year, before
topics are known. Subteams are formed only when they are
needed, by having known topics the full board agrees are important and timely as board business. The executive committee is
formed early, with "super board member" appointments. Subteams are formed with volunteers from the board, thus gaining
participants who are looking for involvement and who are most
interested and knowledgeable about the specific topic at hand.
The executive committee topics usually are selected by the chairperson before board meetings and have some time delay of getting
known to the full board—if they are ever known by the full
board—and even if they are known by the full board, the working
details, knowledge, and power still are within only the executive
committee. Subteams work on predetermined subjects that are
identified by the full board. These subjects are stated with desired
subteam job products and expectations so there are no hidden
agendas or surprises to the full board. Subteams represent a superior solution to leveraging output of the board and give better
measure for truly maximizing the incremental tasks performed by
the full board of directors.

Subteams Leverage Math

Subteams can leverage the strength of a board and, therefore,
greatly increase effectiveness. For example, assume an executive
committee has five members, plus the chairperson, for a total of
six. Now assume these six individuals respond to legitimate board
tasks and all the topics of need during the course of the year. Also
assume that over the course of a year eight key topics arise that
need to be studied and worked on by either the executive committee or a subteam of the board. If volunteers are solicited to

work on these issues through board subteams, the amount of board member effort is leveraged. For those eight issues, say four board members volunteer to work on each of the eight board subteams, that means thirty-two decisions in which members will participate. Thirty-two subteam involvements divided by six executive committee members suggests that board member involvement has been leveraged by a significant factor of more than five.

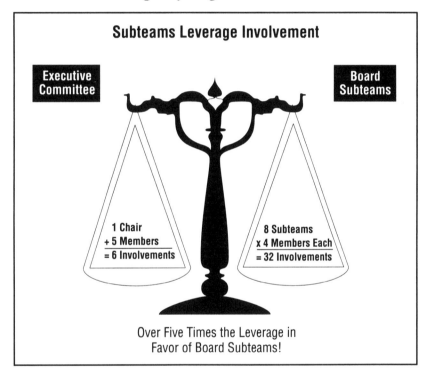

Subteams Leverage Involvement

Executive Committee

Board Subteams

1 Chair
+ 5 Members
= 6 Involvements

8 Subteams
x 4 Members Each
= 32 Involvements

Over Five Times the Leverage in
Favor of Board Subteams!

Characteristics of Effective Teams

In the past, committees were formed. In the future, teams will be formed. Why teams? Teams have proven to be a valuable way to increase the efficiency of people and provisions for progress toward the vision.

Effective and efficient teams can provide progressive, successful accomplishments stemming from their characteristics. Common characteristics and behaviors of teams that function with good results are that they understand and support the vision. When teams come together, they join together to fulfill a common mission or task. While teams are making progress, members of effective teams work at learning—learning to improve their teaming functional skills and interpersonal processes. One of the factors that makes teams so strong is the use of the consensus process for decision making. Strong teams hold meetings to coordinate, schedule, monitor, and to a large extent, solve problems. Teams focus on getting the desired results. Teams then celebrate their accomplishments, and if formed for a temporary, single purpose, they disband when the results are achieved.

Attitudes of Effective Team Members

Effective teams are made up of ordinary people doing extra-ordinary things. Every team culture has norms that determine behavior and serve as a guide to its daily way of life. These norms affect how people work together and communicate, how power and influence are used, how people react to stress, and how people are rewarded. Teams are made up of people who exhibit several special attitudes as part of their culture.

Some common attitudes of team members are that they listen well to others, including not only their own team members but customers, stakeholders, and any others who can affect positive results. Team members openly express their ideas, impressions, and feelings that make visible information and knowledge for success. Effective team members continue to learn and treat learning as a lifelong experience. Effective team members continue to clarify information as they accept assignments and responsibilities. They perform to the best of their abilities, which means that teams actually perform synergistically and yield results of the team beyond what members could ever do independently. Teams model the leadership role and should receive recognition from the authorizing channel that formed the team.

Consensus—The Definition

Teams and effective boards use consensus. Consensus is the process of crafting an agreement all team members will support. Consensus has been achieved when each team member feels heard and understood, at least 70 percent of the team agree they like it—as is—and they will support it as presented, and the other 30 percent of people say they wouldn't present it or write it just that way, but they, too, will support it. To accomplish consensus, rather than voting, the chairperson asks a question, such as, "Is there anyone who can't support this?" When the chairperson does not receive negative feedback to the question, then consensus has occurred.

Often, after a challenging mental merging of thoughts, ideas, and values that are crafted into an agreement that all can support, a special moment in time occurs. This special moment can manifest spontaneous good feelings and positive attitudes of celebration. To let these timely moments of celebration occur can positively strengthen and bolster the team to new heights of satisfaction and morale.

It is good governance for the board to document in policy a statement that consensus will be sought for decisions put before the board and that all members will have an opportunity to present their views. With voting, it is all too common that dominant, assertive members typically express their individual views without full expression from their peers, because some degree of natural intimidation occurs. This diminishes the full human participation benefits to the organization. Consensus should replace the yes and no voting process because this will yield a much stronger deliberation of the board, resulting in more substantial, broad-reaching, and effective decisions for the organization.

Some say it takes too long to gain consensus. Yes, it takes longer to gain consensus than to take a simple vote, but the quality of leadership action is much stronger. If the board is about top-level thinking—and it should be—then rushing through detailed yes or no agenda items is less than ideal and not very effective. The majority-wins style of voting always creates losers, which can decrease motivation, and may foster resentment and bitterness. Quality, consensus-style agenda time should be scheduled for turning values into vision and working through the true job products of the board.

Using the governance model and consensus action is very powerful. Discussions should be focused on what is predefined as board business, and agenda time should be scheduled for board members to talk about decisions, weigh the pros and cons, and compare drafts of language to most favorably affect the whole organization. As a result, the output of consensus deliberations will yield leveraged, effective, and productive results.

Consensus—The Decision-Making Process

The consensus process is a powerful and challenging sequence of decision-making events that contributes to the success of an effective team. Without detailed understanding and mastery of the several important sequential steps of consensus, a board can fall back to the simple discord-creating chore of voting. This has been called majority rules or wins, which also means that the minority loses. A formal consensus process is shown as interpreted from *Rules for Reaching Consensus* (Pfeiffer & Company 1994).

Proposal—The consensus process begins with a written proposal. This written form should be made available to all team members, even before the meeting if possible. The proposal should be presented by one person. It may be helpful to use an overhead projector and transparencies to visually guide the team through the proposal. The facilitator should have at hand blank transparencies and extra marker pens that can be used to help clarify and modify ideas to move the team to consensus.

Clarify Questions—Questions should be made known openly to the whole team so everyone can understand the issues and concerns. The facilitator has the key role of getting the team to communicate. The outcome is not so much answering the questions, but more important, facilitating understanding about the proposal. This is not the time to raise objections; this time should be used to clarify understanding and even make suggestions for improvement, if appropriate.

State Concerns—After the proposal has been outlined and made clear to the team, any pertinent concerns should be addressed. Concerns should be stated and tested for legitimacy by evaluating against the following question: "Is there anything here that would adversely detract from the purpose, vision, and values of the organization?" This phase is time consuming. The facilitator needs to foster a climate that encourages participation. If no major concerns surface, then consensus can be achieved quickly.

First Call for Consensus—At this point, the facilitator may ask, "Have we reached consensus?" If there are no concerns, then the facilitator can declare achievement of consensus. If there are some concerns, but if at least 70 percent like and support the modified proposal as is, and 100 percent will support the modified proposal, then the facilitator can declare achievement of consensus. If there are unresolved concerns, then more work is necessary.

List the Concerns—With unresolved concerns, the next phase is to itemize a list of those concerns and make the list visible to the team. A brainstorming style of responding should be used. This style helps to get to the breadth of thinking of the team without having big speeches for or against any of the items. The facilitator plays a key role in distilling each concern into a short phrase on an overhead transparency or flipchart. This listing helps the team comprehend and keep track of the concerns. The facilitator should use this communication period to aid in team-building momentum. Any concern listed should pass the test of legitimacy. Some validation expressions during this period by the team can be important for growth of the team culture. Concerns tested for legitimacy should be evaluated against the following question: "Is there anything here that would adversely detract from the purpose, vision, and values of the organization?"

Discussion—Now it is important for the team to review, digest, condense, and analyze the list of concerns and issues. With team discussion, all the issues now must be either integrated, merged, removed, or skillfully factored into the resolution proposal. This is challenging and invigorating work for the team and particularly for the facilitator.

If all the concerns are resolved either by removal or integration into the modified proposal, the facilitator can declare achievement of consensus.

Next Call for Consensus—If there are remaining concerns with the modified proposal, the facilitator may now call for consensus. The facilitator may ask, "Can we all support the modified proposal?" If at least 70 percent like and support the modified proposal as is and 100 percent will support the modified proposal, then the facilitator can declare achievement of consensus. If there are unresolved concerns, then more work is necessary.

Evaluate Team Purpose—Unresolved concerns by this point in time should have been thoroughly reviewed for possible integration into the modified proposal. Now the team should elevate its thinking to the overall purpose of the team and ask how this can help filter each of the unresolved concerns.

Clarify Which Values Conflict—The team purpose now should be used as a filter for screening and evaluating unresolved concerns. The team should clarify which concerns are in conflict with the purpose and specifically how they conflict.

Discussion—Now the team should discuss the clarified view of these concerns against the team purpose. With team discussion, all the issues now must be either eliminated as conflicting with team purpose or integrated and merged into a modified proposal because of the team purpose review.

If all the concerns are resolved either by removal or integration into the modified proposal based on the review of the purpose of the team, then the facilitator can declare achievement of consensus.

Next Call for Consensus—If there are remaining concerns with the modified proposal, the facilitator may now call for consensus. The facilitator may ask, "Is there anyone who cannot support the modified proposal?" If at least 70 percent like and support the modified proposal as is, and 100 percent will support the modified proposal, then the facilitator can declare achievement of consensus. If there are still unresolved concerns, then more work is necessary.

Evaluate Motives of Team Members—In some cases, unresolved concerns that remain may have been judged thoroughly and still there is some reason that is preventing resolution. One subtle reason may be the motives of individual team members. At this time, the issue of honesty and trust becomes apparent. Impasse at this point most likely is because of individual motives based on ego or vested interests.

What Is Best for the Team?—To help cut through the problem of self-serving motives, the facilitator should ask, "What is best for the team?" Team members should try to further elevate their thinking as to which of the unresolved concerns really are best for the team.

Discussion—Team trust and individual motives now should become clearer for resolving conflict about remaining concerns. With team discussion, all the issues now must be either eliminated as not valid as best for the team or integrated and merged into a modified proposal to benefit the team.

If all the concerns are resolved either by removal or integration into the modified proposal based on the review of what is best for the team, then the facilitator can declare achievement of consensus.

Last Call for Consensus—If there are remaining concerns with the modified proposal, the facilitator now may call for consensus. The facilitator may ask, "Can we all support the modified proposal?" If at least 70 percent like and support the modified proposal as is and 100 percent will support the modified proposal, then the facilitator can declare achievement of consensus. If there still are unresolved concerns, then only a few options remain.

Closing Options—Time must be allocated to permit the consensus process to work. Many teams will have reached consensus well before moving this far through the process. When major conflict has prevented consensus or time has run out, one of the following options may be exercised at the discretion of the team.

Organize a Subteam—A smaller subteam could be created to do further clarification for the benefit of the full team. In this case, the subteam could be either asked to report back recommendations to the full team or, depending on the nature and timing of the issue, authorized to come to consensus then proceed with implementation.

Conduct a Straw Poll—Consensus *never* takes a vote, but occasionally a nonbinding show of hands can be helpful and make visible the feelings of the team. Some now could be willing to support the unresolved concerns, or if the team is widely split, it could give a clue for withdrawing the proposal.

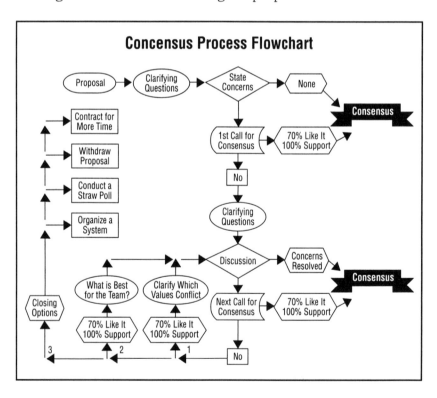

Concensus Process Flowchart

Withdraw the Proposal—At some point in time, the proposal may be judged as impossible to salvage.

Contract for More Time—During the deliberations, the team may run short of time. If this occurs, the team may choose to take time from other agenda items and continue or stop now and pick up the consensus process at the next meeting. Even if only one team member objects then this is not an option.

Consensus—Valuable Team Tool

The team can be one of the most solid and effective entities of human society, and consensus can be a valuable tool of decision making for the team culture. Some tension always is evident as individual team member's needs are balanced with team needs and expectations. Each team member has inherent individual purposes, goals, and needs, and the use of consensus can be a powerful process for huddling the team into common thinking and conformity for support of the mutual purposes and goals of the team. Good teams will build *esprit de corps*. Cultivating this team spirit builds the contagious and spontaneous pride in belonging to the organization.

Chapter 12

Hot Spots

Communications to Transform Values into Vision

An effective board must have effective communications. Board communications occur at various levels. There are five common understandings of communication levels that can occur:

1. Clichés
2. Information
3. Ideas and Opinions
4. Values and Feelings
5. Intimacy and Confession

Each level of communication has a purpose and fulfills a need. An effective board certainly must move beyond the first two levels of communication. But to achieve a higher level of communication, a greater level of trust must be present. The higher the level of trust, the higher the potential level for communication. It takes greater trust to move beyond information sharing. It takes even more trust to share values and feelings. Intimacy requires the highest level of trust.

Too often, boards get only to level two. They share information but don't get much else done. When sufficient trust is present, a board then can begin to share ideas and opinions. An effective board, however, must build trust to the point that level-four communication occurs—communication that involves sharing values and feelings. One key job product of the board is to transform values into vision. Unless the board can achieve understanding and communication, particularly at the "values and feelings" level, how can a board hope to capture and communicate vision for the whole organization?

Board Growth Circle

One way to judge the effectiveness of a board is to observe at what level communication occurs. It may be postulated that a higher level of trust encourages more time spent at higher levels of communication, which yields greater board effectiveness. This may be called the board growth circle.

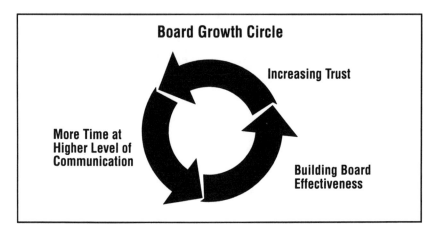

Board Growth Circle

Increasing Trust

More Time at Higher Level of Communication

Building Board Effectiveness

Part of the growth process of any board lies in the teaming development of the people assembled. Any activities, questions, processes, exercises, or agenda items that help increase trust can pay big dividends in growing the communication that results in building an effective board.

Ways to Build Trust

What are some practical ways to build trust? Here are ideas that can be blended into most board cultures as fertilizer to speed and foster growth-building trust.

1. **Begin with Orientation and Training**—Bringing together a new set of board members demands that time be spent on orienting each member on the basics of governance and the job products of the board. As each member comes to understand the roles, responsibilities, job products, and expectations of his or her

position, there is greater and greater opportunity to grow the true level of shared trust.

2. **Hold a Yearly Retreat**—People need time to get to know each other. Early in the fiscal year, it is valuable for the board to gather in, preferably, an off-site location to have general togetherness and get to know each other. Although some "business" must be accomplished, the retreat should provide time for relaxing, talking, eating, and working together to help speed the process of getting to know each other. The better people know each other, the more likely they are to move to the next level of communication.

3. **Share Questions at Each Meeting**—Some board agenda time should be devoted to sharing questions and concerns of board members. The questions may be about what is happening in the organization, special circumstances related to the meetings, or future agenda item suggestions. These questions and comments can be a significant safety valve to help vent any feelings of concern or frustration that could otherwise prevent the growth of trust. A written evaluation form also may be helpful.

4. **Create Linking Opportunities**—Effective boards need to learn how to work together. As needs become apparent for additional board work that should be done, subteams of the board should be created to gather special information or do policy drafts that will be reported later to the full board. These highly focused, short-term, results-oriented subteams of the board can provide wonderful opportunities for board members to get to know each other outside the board room while using their skills, knowledge, and experience for the benefit of the organization.

5. **Accept People with Different Personality Traits**—For those who have studied the different personality traits and perspectives of people, it is no surprise that people have different "chemistry" and think differently. For example, some people are more institutional or product centered, others are more relational or process oriented. Difficulties can occur when people have doubts about their job products or outcomes. Clearly defining the roles, responsibilities, job products, and expected outcomes for

every subordinate group, team, subteam, and especially for the whole board will help greatly in building trust. This also helps leverage diversity and keeps all members involved, regardless of personality types.

6. **Actively Monitor and Expect Trust**—It is a good idea to have a survey at the closing of every board meeting to evaluate the meeting. One survey question should relate to trust. For example, "The meeting was conducted in an atmosphere of trust, acceptance, and respect." Each member should respond by circling one of the following five responses: strongly agree, agree, neither agree or disagree, disagree, or strongly disagree. By assigning points to the categories and keeping track of the feedback over time, it is possible to graph the impressions of the complete board. It is healthy to show year-to-date results at the beginning of each meeting. Openness always helps.

7. **Don't Try to Teach Trust**—Trust can't be taught, it must be grown. It is not a process, but a by-product. It is not a goal, but a result. Trust is not permanent; it is an illusive commodity that requires nurturing. It is an internal perception, an emotion of confidence, an inherent faith, but sometimes it also is a fickle feeling that can vanish quickly when difficulties arise. Trust is something people must desire and expect, but it is something that is more given than taken. It is impossible to build trust directly because if there is reason to talk about it, then there is reason to admit that it is missing. If trust ever becomes an issue, then regardless of how good the monitoring says it is, trust just took a dive. As difficulties are positively resolved through true teamwork, character can be recognized and trust will grow—indirectly—not because of trying to increase it but because of maturing and growing it through visible accomplishments and shared successes.

Ironically, as people new to each other come together, they tend to say they have trust, and surveys show high levels of this innocent beginning trust. Then, as people start to work together, this initial trust usually is significantly diminished. It is not uncommon for surveys to show a drop in trust perceptions after a meeting or two as realism surfaces. Then, as true teambuilding occurs, problem solving is accomplished, and mutual successes and character become visible, people begin to get to really know, understand, and appreciate each other. With a few successes, trust can grow and flourish and become even stronger as new challenges are met and resolved in an open atmosphere of respect.

Steps to an Effective Board

Building an effective board takes patience and persistence. It begins with good meetings and meeting mechanics. It focuses on governance and good governance principles. Then it implements total quality attitudes and continuous improvement.

1. **Schedule Meetings Well in Advance**—Board meetings need to be scheduled far enough in advance so that all board members can reserve space on their calendars and plan to attend. It is a good idea to block out the plans before the beginning of the year so there are no surprises later. High board member attendance at the regularly scheduled meetings is a threshold requirement for boards to be fully effective.

2. **Structure Agendas with Only Board Business**—Board agendas should include only real board business. This is easy to say, but tough to accomplish unless a good tool of governance, such as the governance model, has been applied. The governance model acts as a filter to screen out all nonboard business that can creep onto agendas and detract from accomplishing the job products of the board. Leaders should not be tempted to arbitrarily include in board agendas things such as operational activities, subordinate group whims, general staff items, or missions/goals and "how to" related discussions.

Board agendas need to be clearly focused on achieving the outcomes specified in the job products of the board. Board meetings need to be focused on accomplishing the work of the board, not delegated work. Time should be spent in regularly reviewing and updating, as necessary, various means-related policies, including governance policy and the appropriate job products of the board itself, relationship policy and any organizational- and structure-related questions, and limitations policy with any new or redefined boundaries. The bulk of board meeting time should be focused on clarification of ENDs policy. ENDs policy work includes defining, refining, and clarifying who the organization is, what the vision is, and how success will be realized and recognized when it is achieved.

Every board meeting should be wrapped up with a list of accomplishments of the meeting and a refresher of the vision statement. The following question should be posed: "Were all the accomplishments of this meeting in support of progress toward the vision?" This sensitivity can help keep the board and its leaders focused on the true work of the board.

3. **Cultivate and Implement Good Governance**—Every board must to come to grips with what form of governance will be used. This decision is made by every board, either consciously or by default. Will the governance style be similar to the traditions of the past, will it be sensitive to change, and will it cope with real dynamics of the future? Successful organizations of the future will be increasingly conscious and sensitive to learning about and implementing new concepts, such as the engineered organizational model and the governance model, to build an effective board and an empowered organization and maximize organizational successes.

4. **Develop Efficient Board Communications**—Efficient communications are needed, especially between the board and staff. The chief staff officer should be available at every board meeting for ongoing communications linking. This linking can be done during breaks, over lunches and dinners, as well as during formal time on the meeting agendas.

Most chief staff officers are expected to provide insights into trends and opportunities for the future. Too often, however, a board report can be structured with only a display of various types and forms of information. Unless the report concludes with some meaningful transition into opportunities for discussion, the report will be less than effective.

A good chief staff officer report will lead to some response by the board. It is most useful to craft board reports with a sensitivity to the role and job products of the board itself. A report that is "for your information" should be discarded or submitted as a written and attached report. An effective board report will summarize the key trends, pertinent information, and relative input, then solicit germane discussion and response. This kind of agenda item gets to the heart of the board purpose and should be encouraged and expected from anyone reporting to the board.

5. **Expect Good Board Reports**—The board should accept only high-quality reports. Good board reports have certain common qualities. If the one who reports complains "nobody asked questions about my report," then perhaps the oral report should have been a written report only. If the board comments, "I think board action is appropriate" regarding the XYZ written report, then perhaps it could have been an oral report.

Board reports should be structured to focus on relevant trends and key information that is needed and desirable for the board to have. A good board report should link the information shared with the board directly to the real work to be performed by the board. This link should identify the pertinent board role or specific job product (using accepted terms of governance) so the board can focus quickly on why the subject is being addressed and what work or type of response generally is needed or expected. This means reports should be given primarily when a board response is needed and appropriate. Monitoring information, for example, is better attached to the agenda to be read by board members unless targets are not being achieved and some board action is fitting. As this linking is performed by the presenter, it should become obvious to the board during the discussion as to what kind of response would be appropriate. A presentation is most effective when the presenter "owns" the materials for the presentation. A canned speech—one that is written so that any "talking head" can deliver it—can be detected by an audience within the first few seconds. Under these conditions, the material is not presented as well as it could have been.

Take the situation of two different speakers. In the first example, a report is crafted with visuals that contain a few key concepts, and the speaker elaborates with stories and personal experiences that establish an instant connection with the listeners. In the second example, a report is prepared with detailed and artistic visuals and is presented with a professionally created synchronized script.

For the first speaker, rapport was instant, the knowledge imparted was personalized, the communication was in "real time," the remarks were candid, and the communication was effective. It offered a striking contrast to the second speaker, whose approach was premeditated, impersonal, disingenuous, and less verbally communicative. The second speech could have been provided more effectively as a written report. A good rule of thumb is that if material is prepared and there is a search for someone to present it, then this material probably should be submitted as a written report. If the presenter has not been personally involved in preparing the speech or if the presenter is not comfortable with representing and presenting the subject, this also probably should be a written report.

An effective board has leaders who are sensitive to structuring quality presentations so that board agendas efficiently maximize use of board time and quickly get to the level of communication needed to obtain the most progressive responses for the greatest organizational results and gains.

6. **Keep Minutes Simple**—Minutes should be used to document the official record of what occurred during the board meeting. While minutes are intended to record the time, date, place, who was present, and the official actions taken by the board, they should be kept relatively simple and refer to other documents as necessary. For example, much of the work of the board should be reflected in board policy revisions, amendments,

improvements, clarifications, and changes, so for matters of policy it is important to let the policy manual carry the load of tracking board progress. The most significant outcomes from board meetings ideally are reflected in key policy language clarifications and improvements that are not necessary to totally reproduce in minutes because copies of policy can be merely attached. It is not a good idea to record who made certain comments during the meeting because, whether the consensus or voting process is used, these comments, whether positive or negative, will only detract from the holism of the board. Good positive minutes need only state that consensus was reached.

7. **Use Total Quality**—In his book *The Only Thing That Matters*, Karl Albrecht says, "The only thing that matters in business is delivering customer value." To deliver the customer value expected by customers of the future means implementing total quality principles. There are great leaders, such as W. Edwards Deming, Joseph M. Juran, and Philip B. Crosby, who have influenced modern thinking on quality. While their prescriptions are

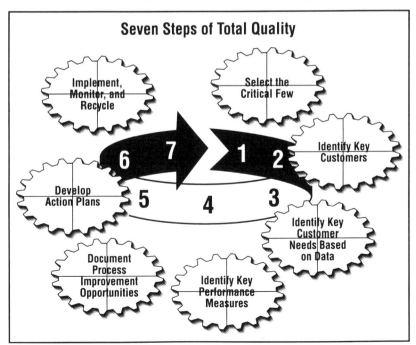

powerful, it is important to select a total quality process that works for you. A helpful total quality process map popular at the Society of Automotive Engineers and shown on page 129 describes seven steps necessary for delivering "the only thing that matters."

The process begins with the selection of the critical few. Although this model is applicable throughout the whole organization at all levels to meet customers' needs, in the case of the board, this means selecting the critical few ENDs for the organization to work toward. Next, it is imperative to identify who the customers are. This may involve demographics and prioritizing of selected groups or users. Without this step, it is hopeless to proceed to the next step. Once the customers are identified, customer needs must be documented. It is imperative that customers be asked so there is no confusion. This basic input supports the development of knowledge-based solutions identified to truly meet customer expectations. Closely related to needs identification is the documentation of performance measures and the associated key processes. This is where key customer needs are translated into customer satisfaction requirements and processes are structured to meet those requirements. Next, it is important to document opportunities for process improvement. This involves analysis, simplification, prioritization, and optimization to achieve the greatest results. Once the processes are organized, action plans must be developed; problems resolved; and solutions, outcomes, and deadlines established. The cycle is completed with the implementation and monitoring of the results against original customer expectations. Then, the cycle is repeated for the next issue judged to be of the critical few. This process is targeted to achieve quality in meeting or exceeding customer expectations while delivering superior value to all stakeholders of the organization.

8. **Evaluate Board Governance Results**—What is good governance? How is good governance recognized? How can governance be evaluated? These are all questions that should be investigated by a board. One way to understand the mechanics of governance is to evaluate board members to see how they rate the

level of current governance. An evaluation questionnaire is provided in the appendix to help answer these questions. This questionnaire can serve as a tool to document current governance satisfaction. More important, it can be used to provide an annual means to benchmark progress in governance growth. It is important to keep track and monitor the progress of good governance building. This should become an area of board monitoring to ensure governance progress is made annually. Good governance can be the single greatest factor propelling organizational successes for the future.

9. **Improve Continuously**—There is no greater need in the modern business environment than to continuously improve. Teams of people must become learners—always seeking to apply the best technology for problem solving. Edward Johnson III, chair and chief executive officer of Fidelity Investments made this insightful comment: "We have seen the future and its name is technology. The way we use it will determine how successful we are. The winners won't necessarily be companies with leading-edge systems. Nor will the losers be those with old technology. The prize, instead, will go to those who learn how to use technology most creatively." Effective boards are never stationary but are continuing to improve and are fostering attitudes of continuous improvement among the breadth and depth of the total organization.

Chapter 13

Program Life

Program Life Understanding

For an organization to be effective, resources must be used effectively throughout all stages of the program life for every product and service provided by the organization. Each product and service will move through its stages of program life, including development, mature productivity, and declining use. Good leadership will recognize program life and apply all available provisions and resources to create and supply products and services (shown on the engineered organizational model) to meet customer needs. New and ongoing programs are processes that require the use of these provisions. Because every product and service is in some stage of its program life, leadership must know the respective stages so resource allocations can be maximized. Understanding program life and effective leadership can affect the provisions cog of the engineered organizational model significantly. How an organization treats programs psychologically can affect, either positively or negatively, the effectiveness of the organization. Better understanding of program life can result in improvements in applying the organization's financial resources.

The products and services of any organization should be designed to meet the desires and expectations of those who use them, while sustaining the supplying organization. These organizations generally begin with noble intentions but too often continue well beyond their usefulness. Organizations periodically and regularly should analyze, identify, and phase out programs that are no longer beneficial.

Transformation of Knowledge

The purpose of an organization is to gather sufficient input, transform ideas, and create useful output for use by customers. The customer must become involved increasingly earlier in the process so that all the needs are identified clearly and documented. Only then can the organization work to transform those ideas into some form of useful reality. Once the output is available, the customer can have full benefit of the features requested, desired, planned, and expected. The service the organization provides is the added value of applying the knowledge of the people of the organization combined with the appropriate use of the provisions and policy.

In today's world, change is driving complexity and is demanding the operation processes of successful organizations to speed up at an increasingly faster rate. Because the outputs of an organization must occur on this faster scale of productivity, there is need for continued increased efficiencies that eliminate the nonessen-

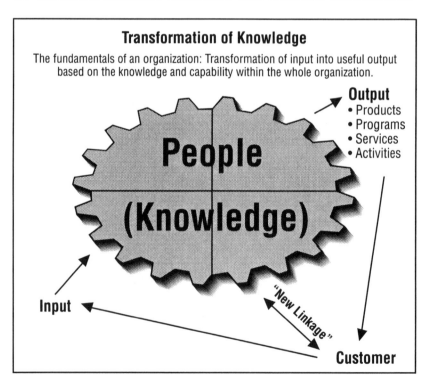

Transformation of Knowledge

The fundamentals of an organization: Transformation of input into useful output based on the knowledge and capability within the whole organization.

People (Knowledge)

Output
- Products
- Programs
- Services
- Activities

Input

"New Linkage"

Customer

tials and focus leverage to achieve maximum gains. Inefficiencies too often go unnoticed and remain hidden. The future demands that an effective approach be in place to watch for, seek out, and recognize these areas.

Information Trend—New Linkage

With progress into the information age, the value of an organization is growing beyond the products and services that have been provided traditionally. Increasingly, customers want to have access to and use of raw information from internal data bases that has been previously available only under controlled conditions from within the organization. Wise and successful organizations of the future will learn to create a new linkage and connect the customer more directly for mutual benefit in ways beyond the traditional input and formal output. Increasingly, the customer wants to have access to the data base of information. In this case, the customer can most effectively do the transforming of information into yet other products and services for the customer's benefit. An example of this information age data transfer is the use of membership rosters. Although unheard of a few years ago, now it is common for organizations to merchandise CD ROM (compact disk, read-only memory) data bases as products to meet the needs of customers.

Stages of a Program Life

The program life concept model features three stages: developmental, mature, and declining. Typically, organizations always will need resources for developing new programs, continuing mature programs, and looking out for declining programs that can sponge away valuable resources.

Developmental Programs

A healthy organization should have developmental programs at a volume of some 10 percent to 15 percent of the total programs offered. Developmental programs help organizations demonstrate progress. Organizations should be open to new and progressive ways of meeting customer needs without becoming impractical and overly enamored with the jazzy, exciting, and trendy products and services that are not feasible to ever become future core and mature programs. At the same time, good leadership requires a healthy balance of all new opportunities with wholesome risk so that true and realistic future progress is ensured.

Key Questions for Knowledge Gathering

Organizations need to develop new programs with the benefit of good knowledge-based decision making. It is helpful to preconsider the questions that should be asked in strategizing for the future. For example, in the presence of potential customers and stakeholders, what types of questions can provide the best input into the knowledge base for decision making? The following questions may be used to tickle the imagination and learn of mutual opportunities. These questions are posed in such a way as to focus on the future and help bring to the surface and determine what is most important.

1. What are the three or four most significant opportunities and challenges you face for the future?
2. If you could be provided any program or service that you could use, attend, receive, network to, etc., no matter what, what would provide you the most benefit?
3. Is there a problem you currently are having that you are not getting any help with from anyone anywhere?

Valid responses to these questions can provide vital input into current realities about the evolving dynamics of the customers and the marketplace. They can improve greatly the results of future development program selection.

Mature Programs

Mature programs represent the current stability of the organization, and therefore, they typically make up 70 percent to 80 percent of the total programs. These are valuable programs for an organization and its customers. They are the mature programs, where customers' needs are most solidly being met and the return on investment offers positive gains for the organization. For these programs, everybody generally is happy and only routine continuous improvement is needed. The long-term viability of an organization lies in its ability to continue offering these successful and financially viable programs. A highly productive organization continually will be bringing programs into this realm and will have this group of mature programs as a proportionally larger workload than all others. Overall, it is best to do fewer things but to do those things of higher value to the target customer segments. Good business sense is helpful to determine those selected programs that make the most sense for moving toward the vision for the organization.

Declining Programs

There will be programs that have lost the desired effect on the end customer and that are no longer meeting customers' needs. Either the needs have changed, other factors have changed, or these programs just are no longer necessary. For whatever reasons, every organization has some declining programs, but too often, these are not dealt with.

Without some conscious actions, these declining programs will continue in some low-profile and increasingly inefficient way. Declining programs are insidious in nature. Sometimes they are difficult to recognize. Sometimes they are difficult to even consider because of traditions and paradigm values that cloud the issues. Sometimes they are sentimental to the people involved, particularly to those inside the organization. When these declining programs are recognized and appropriate actions are taken, great improvements can be realized.

Some programs can be canceled when it is determined that the need no longer exists. When the need still exists, but the need can be met in new and more efficient ways, then some programs can be combined with other programs to remain efficient. If selected programs are used by fewer and fewer people, then it may be possible to combine these programs to continue to meet most of the interim expectations while creating a softer way to reduce the impact. Good leaders always will be on the alert for exposing these declining programs. The future demands action for operations to be effective, efficient, and successful.

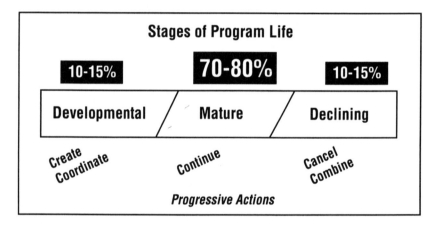

Encourage Those Tough Questions

Successful organizations need to develop new programs, continue mature programs, and cancel or combine declining programs with the benefit of good knowledge-based decision making.

Although the details of programs are not board work, the board needs to encourage those who do manage programs. Tough questions need to be asked and appropriate responses identified.

- What new programs should be started?
- What programs are mature, but strong and useful?
- How can these mature programs be streamlined, continuously improved, and grown even more to ensure long-term viability?

- What programs are declining?
- What programs should be trimmed?
- What programs should be combined for improving efficiency?

Understanding the realistic stages of program life can benefit leaders at all levels of the organization to be on the alert for optimizing the provisions and resources available.

Chapter 14

Fiscal Accountability

Board Budget Approval—The Tradition

An effective board needs to exercise stable fiscal accountability. Tradition suggests that approval of the annual budget by the board of directors delineates organizational authority and demonstrates the epitome of required financial stewardship.

Boards have been trained to look forward to the annual presentation of the budget because of its major significance and relative importance for documenting organizational plans. Budgets tend to highlight what programs are important and how resources will be prioritized and applied to means-oriented activities for the months ahead. Approval of the budget, therefore, has served as a prime method of communicating the specific intentions and priorities for the coming year.

Although the budget is a special tool of management, too often it has become an automatic part of the board processes without good examination as to why. An effective board periodically should contemplate and reconsider how organizational priorities are communicated in view of good governance.

Yes, it is imperative for the board of directors to establish rigid financial controls for the organization, but the effective board should not get caught in the minutiae so often associated with budget approval. An effective board of directors always will be seeking to provide leadership and direction through efficient and creative communication linkage and be ever sensitive to avoiding misplaced focus.

Why Board Budget Approval?

Most literature describing the work of boards teach intimacy between the board and the budget. In *The Nonprofit Organization* by Thomas Wolf, reference is made to the work of the board of directors (called "the trustees"). This reference says: "Approving the budget is not enough. The trustees are responsible for monitoring and if necessary, amending the budget throughout the year." This traditional perspective calls for the board to not only approve the initial budget but to be intimately involved with modifications, large and small, throughout the year. In this case, the board tries to assume the impractical, "eagle eye," step-by-step control of all the detailed processes within the organization.

In *Nonprofit Boards: A Practical Guide to Roles, Responsibilities, and Performance,* Diane J. Duca says: "A budget is more than a set of dollar figures submitted for board approval; it is a fiscal policy tool." In this concept, the budget is not only approved by the board, it also serves as a policy tool that is approved and managed by the board. The budget is a tool, but is it policy and should it be managed by the board? Perhaps this tool is better left in the hands of those managers of the organization who can work more efficiently for the greatest gains rather than having the highest select group of the organization—the board—tinkering at regular or irregular intervals with this fiscal tool called the budget.

The Real Needs

The traditional board budget approval action has evolved over the years as a process to fulfill needs. Those needs were for the board to (1) exercise organizational authority, (2) establish priorities for direction setting, and (3) communicate the board's leadership. Board budget approval does seem to meet these needs. It demonstrates the power of organizational authority because it is the board that is involved. Because special programs are funded through the budget, approval expresses the desired priorities and direction of the board. Once the budget is approved, it also tends to serve as a special communication that shows board commitment to programs through approved funding.

Implementing the engineered organizational model and the governance model can help to meet these needs in direct and optimum ways:

1. Organizational authority of the board is visibly denoted through leadership, with expressed values and vision documented in board policy.
2. Priorities and direction are established by the board through documented vision policy with clarifying ENDs statements.
3. Board communication is optimized by encouraging an empowered organization, not a stifled one that requires detailed approvals.

With good governance, board budget approvals become an unnecessary, detailed, time-consuming, throttling redundancy.

Board Fiscal Behavior

The governance model does not recognize any net incremental value of the board approving or managing an annual budget. In fact, any annual budget approval process by the board generally has a net negative impact on the organization. Because this concept deviates from traditional thinking, it is worthwhile to describe pertinent aspects and problems associated with board budget approval. Most budgets are prepared by either staff or the designated finance committee. By asking for board approval of the annual budget, one of two things will occur. Either the board will become detail experts, plunge into the stipulated specifics, and expect adjustments to line item number 23, and so forth, or they will rubber stamp the proposal as presented. Either case is a lose/lose situation for the board and the organization.

If the board dives into the details of an annual budget, and selected members of the board cause changes (through their thorough knowledge of the organizational operation in some specific areas) on the way toward budget approval, this detracts from the board holism and macro ownership of the organization. Although this approach at first blush appears to provide intimate control—and it does—this control creates major roadblocks to an empowered organization. On the other hand, if a board rubber stamps the budget, this also is unacceptable because good governance leaves no room for this behavior.

Board Budget Approval Causes Inefficiencies

When a board approves a budget by whatever chosen process, this locks in a specific set of budget figures for the year—or at least until the next revision. This causes the following roadblocks and organizational inefficiencies:

1. **Stifles Progressive Thinking.** The image of the budget approved by the board is that these figures are carved in stone. Even if the board encourages flexibility, these figures, once approved, are deemed by the organization to be the ideal, the model, the phoenix, or the standard that is not to be questioned or altered, but achieved. When opportunities come along, they may not even be recognized. Typically, action is not considered because the new opportunity is not included in the approved budget. Furthermore, if some opportunity is recognized, it may be just too much trouble, too untimely, too cumbersome, or too embarrassing to go back to the board requesting appropriate changes. These typical situations will prevent an otherwise good organization from responding to real opportunities that lie ahead.

2. **Lengthens Response Time.** If a well-grounded beneficial adjustment is needed to the approved budget, for whatever courageous rationale, it must wait until a future board meeting and compete with other hot topics to find a place on the agenda. Frankly, many opportunities will be missed because of this lethargic budget approval process.

3. **Removes Control from the Best Managers.** Those closest to the pertinent level of detail are best at managing the

budget for their respective area of control. Having several people, particularly at the highest levels of the organization, involved in the details of the budget approval process guarantees that control is removed from those who should be most capable for their area. The process of bringing the budget to the board level only weakens and detracts from overall organizational leadership.

4. **Diminishes Board Leadership.** When a board spends time on details, including things such as scrutinizing and approving the figures of the annual budget, it trivializes board leadership. This activity of budget approval provides too much focus on "how" rather than "what" for creating visions of the future and reduces the overall effectiveness of board leadership.

5. **Detracts from Governance Policy Focus.** One of the job products of the board is to provide written policy to lead and guide the organization. It is relevant to recognize that discussions by the board on specific budget figures always are guided by policy—whether written or unwritten. Also, time spent on the budget yields approved detailed budget figures and rarely yields any documented policy clarification with pertinent rationale. So, private board time spent on budget details inevitably involves policy, but this time spent on the budget detracts from the board spending more productive time clarifying and documenting the specific policies that are applicable.

Why not start from the beginning and bypass the sluggish hierarchy of budget approval by the board? If designated managers are empowered to manage the budget, more positive results can be achieved for the fast-changing future. An effective board will prioritize time for leadership—time for clarifying and documenting policy representing the values of the organization applicable to the numerous pertinent issues rather than spending time on decision making on event-specific, means-oriented, budget-related figures.

Good Fiscal Governance Defined

A progressive board that is exercising leadership for an empowered organization will predetermine the criteria for an acceptable budget and delegate the management of the budget to others. A good board has no self-imposed job product prerogative to scrutinize and manage annual budget figures. With the governance model, the board of directors has no need to perform the traditional duty of approving an annual budget.

An effective board that is exercising the engineered model will (1) establish and maintain fiscal governance policy permitting an empowered organization that yields expedient application and management of all resources and (2) monitor fiscal progress through succinct measures of ENDs progress along with selected pertinent financial measures.

A finance committee may be created to more closely define and work the budget issues. The specified job products of a finance committee could include preparing, managing, and cultivating the budget. The board does not need to take an active role in approving the annual budget.

Criteria for Good Fiscal Governance

An effective board will work to predefine the key criteria that delineate good budget characteristics and good fiscal governance for the organization. These criteria for financial stability should be documented in limitations policy. Because limitations policies establish limits for what is acceptable to the board, documenting these boundaries is all that is required for creating an environment for empowerment. There are a few key elements of financial policy the board should document to provide definition and understanding to an empowered organization. These can be captured in a few lines in a relatively simple policy format. Some typical phrases of criteria could include the following.

No Negative Net Earnings. Boards need to establish basic expectations for financial stability. One common criterion that establishes an essential concept is that expenses shall not exceed income. Positive net earnings for the year demonstrate fiscal responsibility and stability. Although this is a simple notion, it is fundamental for the design of an annual budget. Some organizations stipulate that earnings shall not be less than a specified minimum positive net earnings target for the year. This will cause growth in the organizational net worth each year and contribute to fiscal stability. Positive net earnings and net worth growth are challenging to accomplish, but these certainly are not illegal, even for not-for-profit organizations. A minimum positive net earnings can be expressed as a minimum return on equity, return on assets, or net earnings ratio as desired.

No Unacceptable Risk. It is appropriate to stipulate some philosophy about risk. The degree of optimism or the degree of conservatism always plays a role in budget design. It may be acceptable for a board to state that financial estimates should be based only on conservative estimates. The board might feel more comfortable with words like "financial conditions that jeopardize the fiscal stability for effective and prudent operations are not permitted." In this case, it could be sufficient to let the organization apply reasonable interpretations of the words "conservatism", "jeopardize", and "prudent". If the board becomes uncomfortable with these policies for whatever reasons, it may wish to detail the boundaries.

No Use of Funds Deviating from Board Policy. The budget should be developed consistent with the direction for the organization as described in the ENDs policy. For example, a policy may state, "No budgeting shall deviate appreciably from organizational priorities as expressed in ENDs policies of the board." The products and services as funded in the budget should maximize progress and support the overall vision for the organization.

No Intermingling of Funds. The organization should not have the freedom to arbitrarily move funds from one account to another. For example, the board may choose to restrict that "foundation funds and/or other financial funds cannot be commingled with operational finances."

These items are examples of criteria that an effective board should predetermine as unacceptable boundaries for overall fiscal stability and the budget. Therefore, if budgets meet all the prescribed criteria the board has developed and documented, then those budgets would, in fact, be approved if they were presented to the board. The power of the proactive governance model is that once the board predetermines boundary criteria along with vision, the organization instantly is empowered for progress. For the board to spend time on approval of the annual budget figures is both a waste of valuable board time and a disempowerment of the total capability of the organization.

Monitoring for Fiscal Stability

The board should proactively communicate direction and leadership to the organization while monitoring the progress in all areas, including the important selected financial measures. The following represents a few key measures that could be routinely provided to the board for monitoring fiscal stability. The board should document in relationship policy (on monitoring subordinate group performance) the preferences on the methods and frequencies of monitoring parameters of organizational performance. Then, as the board monitors organizational performance, any time the fiscal parameters the board has chosen to monitor become out of bounds or beyond expectations, the board can and should exercise whatever resources are deemed appropriate to rectify the matter.

Return on Equity

One powerful ratio the board may wish to monitor is the return on equity (ROE). In this ratio, the ROE is calculated by dividing the net earnings for the year, which is the total cash flow for the year, by the average net worth for the year. The net earnings is the total unrestricted income or revenue minus the total expenses for all activities from operations, development, and general investments, if any. The average net worth can be defined as the initial net worth at the beginning of the year, plus the final net worth at the end of the year divided by two. The board may decide that net worth calculations should not count any foundation funds. The board may choose to request a regular monitor reporting of the ROE progress during the year as a year-to-date status for each board meeting. The figure shows an example of a type of ROE monitoring. The year-to-date figure can be misleading because an organization often will have known waves of income and expenses. The best figure for board monitoring of ROE is the figure projected for the year.

Return on Assets

The monitoring of total return on total assets (ROA) is another gauge of financial condition. This is the ratio of net earnings (or net income) divided by the total assets. It is a measure of the income generated from the total assets (or total resources) of the organization. The ratio is expressed as a percent; the higher the ratio, the better the ROA, and the greater efficiency of the organization to create earnings. Assets usually are available because borrowed finances and loans have been used to provide and fund the assets. This means that earnings must be used to pay back the liabilities with interest. Therefore, as is true with all individual measures, monitoring ROA is an important but insufficient measure because it gives no clue as to the debt load of the organization. To determine the amount of assets funded by debt, it is useful to also view the debt-to-asset ratio. It is prudent to monitor a few selected financial measures as a group of measures (rather than using a single one) to concurrently determine the financial stability of the organization.

Total Net Worth

Another example of financial monitoring relates to the total net worth. Boards should be aware of this financial information as an indication of the financial stability of the organization. It is not good for an organization to try to survive from month to month without equity. Even a not-for-profit organization should build some net worth for fiscal stability. The board may choose to determine a desired minimum to provide sustainable stability and, therefore, expect an annual growth in net worth until that level is achieved. Also, a targeted ceiling level of equity can be identified so that earnings can be optimized to give the membership the best value for the products and services provided by the organization rather than arbitrarily just growing the net worth equity. The change in net worth is another way to quickly observe if the revenues are exceeding the expenses for a financially stable organization.

Current Ratio

Another method of monitoring is with the current ratio. This is the ratio of current assets to current liabilities. The current ratio provides an indication of the ability of the organization to pay its bills during the year. It shows the general availability of cash to pay off the liabilities (debts) as they come due. A current ratio of 1.0 means that for every dollar of short-term debt there is a dollar of assets available to cover the debt. A current ratio of 2.0 means that for every dollar of short-term debt there are two dollars of liquid assets available. The more conservative the organization, the higher the current ratio. If an organization is dependent on loans, then this ratio can be of more importance because banking institutions like to see a current ratio of 1.5 to 2.0 as an indication of solvency. If an organization is financially secure and not dependent on borrowing, then more funds can be kept in long-term investments to help maximize earnings.

Total Debt-to-Asset Ratio

Another way to view the fiscal strength of the organization is with the total-debt-to-total-asset ratio. This measure shows how much of the assets are funded by debt. It indicates the percentage of debt the organization has, as compared to the amount of total assets. The higher the percentage, the more leveraged the organization is, and the lower the percentage, the more conservative the organization is. Leveraged organizations gain funding from borrowing, and conservative organizations have funding from cash flow of operations. The board may choose to adopt an acceptable zone for debt-to-asset percentage that represents the degree of leverage determined to be fitting.

Asset Turnover Ratio

The asset turnover ratio is the amount of revenue divided by the total assets. With this parameter, it is possible to evaluate the efficiency of the organization at generating revenue with the assets or resources available. This ratio can vary from as low as 0.2 to over 2.0. The higher the ratio, the more efficient the organization. The board may want to determine an acceptable zone for asset turnover ratio based on historic experience and desired performance.

Net Income to Total Income

The net income to total income is a ratio that describes the percentage of funds kept as net earnings compared with the total income. The higher the percentage, the greater the amount of funds available to the organization to pay back debt or increase the net worth. The board may wish to determine an acceptable zone and stipulate positive earnings. The acceptable region can be anywhere from just greater than zero up to higher levels of 10 percent to 15 percent for very high-performing organizations.

Revenue per Employee

One last financial monitoring chart shows the revenue per employee. When plotted showing the historic progress, this chart can reveal the productivity gains (or losses) for the entire organization. Although, in any given year, productivity can be up or down in dollars per employee, it is a healthy indication of progress of the organization for this trend to be on a substantially positive slope.

Financial Auditing

An effective, disciplined board should have provisions for additional internal financial auditing. For example, a financial audit committee or audit team, separate from the finance committee, should be established to provide an alternative source for monitoring. This team should actively audit the financial health along with the accounting methods used within the organization. The major job products of the financial audit team should be to first select an outside independent financial auditor and, later, to meet with that auditor to review the results of the internal inspection and evaluate the internal accounting controls.

The outside auditor should audit the financial statements of revenues, expenses, cash flows, and net worth for the most recently ended fiscal year before the results are published in an annual report format. Ideally, the results of the audit should conclude that the financial statements are free of misstatements and fairly represent the fiscal position of the organization. Additionally, the audit should conclude that the processes and procedures used were in accordance with generally accepted accounting standards and principles. The audit should reveal whether internal accounting controls provide satisfactorily thorough audit trails and sufficient details.

Although some continuity of using the same auditor for a few years can be beneficial, especially if changes and improvements are necessary along the way to improve the accounting systems, it also is a good idea to change auditors every few years to provide fresh insights and ensure complete neutrality in the auditing process.

Summary on Fiscal Accountability

There are many options for financial inputs and ratios beyond those shown here to help evaluate the financial health of an organization. However, it is important that the board select only those few measures that supply enough insight about the fiscal stability of the organization to give assurances to the board of acceptable progress. Sometimes it is useful to compare the organization's financial status not only against historic performance of the organization but to compare with sister organizations and perhaps similar or competing organizations as well.

One word of caution: It is important that the board monitor enough to determine financial stability and overall fiscal performance, but the board should take care not to arbitrarily intrude into the duties and day-to-day operations of the chief staff officer. If, through monitoring, the financial performance is deemed unacceptable—without sufficient reasons or justification—then the board has grounds for taking further actions to correct the situation. Monitoring selected parameters should be designed to provide the board with enough early warning of any significant financial deficiencies to have response time for corrective actions.

Chapter 15

Development Funds

What Are Development Funds?

Development funds are an important segment of the provisions cog of the engineered organizational model. Too often, they are not recognized and considered by not-for-profit organizations. Development funds can be likened to the vital research and development spending allocations of for-profit corporations. An effective board must provide assurances that sufficient funds for development are in fact set aside and earmarked for this purpose. Also, an effective board must ensure that a process is in place for properly selecting the most appropriate projects for leading the organization toward the vision of the future.

ENDs statements of the organization easily answer the questions "what good?" and "for whom?," but the question "at what cost?" is more challenging to define and often is left unstated. By ensuring development resources and development cost allocations are properly in place, an effective board can demonstrate responsibility at fulfilling the commitment to provide leadership for moving toward the vision. Too often, the overall financial focus is only on short-term, day-to-day activities, so sound financial planning related to longer term development funds is rigorously needed to ensure continued vigor and long-range success.

How Much Funding Should Be Applied?

Every organization needs to have an eye toward the future and commit resources for moving toward the vision. Long-term success at meeting future customer needs is what is at risk. It is healthy for some proportion of the organizational effort to be focused on

155

growing new products and services for tomorrow. A key question is: What degree of financial commitment is appropriate for this development?

The answer depends largely on (1) the organization's current respective fields of endeavors, (2) current financial stability and strength, and (3) general overall commitment to future growth. For most organizations, the amount of development funding should be similar to corporate research and development spending and fall as a minimum between 2 percent to 5 percent of the annual revenue budget. However, development funding can be nearly twice that much for those dynamic organizations that need faster change or expect entrance into new markets sooner. The board needs to come to grips with a specific personalized answer to this question as applied to your organization if it hasn't already. Some stretch-expectations exhibited in this commitment to development funding can pay large dividends for the future.

What Is a Development Project?

Definitions are important, particularly so everyone involved in the leadership has a similar concept of what is included and expected. A development project can be defined as a funded or financially subsidized expansion or trial entrance into a product, process, or service that investigates, fosters, and demonstrates the viable feasibility of progress toward the vision, with favorable consequential membership benefits for current and/or new members of the future.

Development projects should be funded from a development project budget allocation. Usually these kinds of projects require special resources because they are too significant to just be absorbed by normal day-to-day operations. Even with significant, continuous improvement activities, an organization often will fall short in key areas of development unless provisions are established for development projects. Because allocated funding is needed, development projects each must stand on its own merits and be evaluated against other ideas so the strongest and highest priority projects can be selected and funded.

Proposed development projects can cover a wide variety of possibilities, including (1) expanded activities, (2) studies, or even (3) trial entrances into new programs and services. These can range from establishing new computer technologies for improved services and modernization to creating a whole new arm of the organization to meet the needs of an expanded new membership base.

Development projects should be aimed initially at areas where project leaders can investigate, foster, and demonstrate feasibility of the new or expanded product, process, or service. The projects should exhibit measurable progress toward the vision of the organization while becoming a viable and significant benefit for current members and/or new members of the future. It is a good idea to predetermine measures for tracking progress of the project. Monitoring the progress is a discipline that can pay big dividends.

Development Project Requests

An organization needs to have a process and cycle for causing the board and subordinate groups of the organization to be thinking about and proposing new and creative development projects that can better meet customer needs and give the organization vigor in future years. These ideas and possibilities should be documented. A standard and simple development project request form can help apply consistency to documentation.

The input form should begin with basic information about the project: the name of the project, the name of the project champion, the staff coordinator, and the name of the requesting part of the organization, which typically will be a proactive subordinate group. It is a good idea to identify the project champion (member) and supporting staff person to help lead the team from the requesting responsible subordinate group. This team should be influential to help assemble the input, define the plans, surface the merits, provide support, and help sell the proposed development project idea.

The form should include various fundamental information needed by those who decide which projects actually receive the funding and which ones do not—assuming there are more proposed project funds requested than there are development funds to be allocated. As shown on the sample form, it is helpful to have the purpose and goals of the project clearly visible. The form should indicate the purpose of the program, service, process, or activity and list the major supporting goals. It should show benefits and describe the feasibility of this to become a major membership benefit and potentially a core function to the organization for the future.

The financial specifics include the annual revenues, expenses, and development fund costs for the project. From this information,

---

Development Project Request

Project Name: _____

Project Champion: _____

Staff Coordinator: _____

Responsible Subordinate Group: _____

Purpose
What is the purpose of this program, service, process, or activity?

Goals
List the major goals that show benefits and demonstrate the feasibility of this to become a core function of this organization.

Cash Flow	Year #1	Year #2	Year #3	Year #4	Year #5
Revenue	5000	7000	9000	10000	11000
Expense	15000	15000	7000	0	0
Dev. Fund Cost	10000	8000	(2000)	(10000)	(11000)

Background
What special information helps explain this endeavor and why it is important?

Significant Milestones
List the major milestones planned showing what must be accomplished each year.

Progress Report on Milestones
For multiyear funded projects, list what results have been completed.

it is possible to tell not only the requested development cost for this year, but the projected annual amount required, along with how long it will take for this project to be completed or self-sustaining.

The next section should contain special information that helps explain the specifics of this endeavor and why it is important. Additionally, the form should show a list of the major milestones planned and what must be accomplished for each successive year. For multiyear funded projects, it is helpful to provide a list of what results already have been completed to give credibility and strength of argument for continuing the work at the levels of financial support requested.

Development Project Process

Every organization needs to give attention to a process for development projects. The process should include three phases, including identification, selection, and implementation.

Project Identification Phase

The project identification phase begins with a call for development project proposals from subordinate groups of the organization. The board may want to have some communication involvement here to ensure the subordinate groups are giving sufficient consideration to the conception of good ideas for the future.

Subordinate groups should understand the definition of the development projects and have a clear view of what kind of project is appropriate. Proposed projects should be documented on the development project form and submitted to the team that was formed to mediate the selection process.

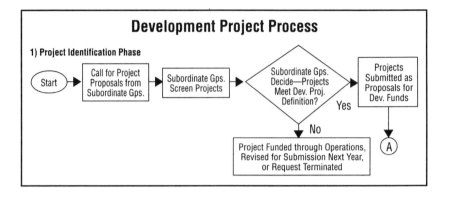

Project Selection Phase

Once the input is gathered, a meeting can be called to select development projects for the year. Who decides which proposed projects should be funded? Every organization must answer that question. It could be the board of directors itself because this is important work and decisions made here will affect the organization for the future. At the same time, the board may choose to delegate this work to a development project selection team or committee. The members of this team could come from the board, past officers, or members of key subordinate groups. Because this is an annual ongoing process, the board may wish to establish a relationship policy that designates the composition, scope/authority, and job products for establishing the development project team or committee.

Once the committee or team is established, team members should meet for the purpose of project selection. In preparing for the meeting, the proposals should be collected and compiled into a briefing manual for the selection team members. This briefing manual should be sent to team members before the meeting to allow the members to become familiar with the proposals. In addition, the selection team members should be asked to individually rate the proposed development projects (continued and new projects together) and send their results to the staff or team leader for compilation. The development project selection matrix form is a useful analysis tool for helping to quantify the relative strength of each project proposal. The summary of this input can be called a round one ranking of the projects. It is a good way to identify the projects all team members believe are most important. For example, this input can be assembled into a ranking from highest to lowest priority and used as beginning ranking for the meeting. The purpose of the meeting of this development project selection team, then, is to reach consensus on the selected list of projects that receive funding for the year within the ceiling limit.

Once the selection team has gathered for its meeting, some members may have questions and may appreciate further understanding of the proposed development projects. Before the initial round one ranking is revealed, all the project champions should provide a brief monitoring report for those continuing projects and introduce any new project proposals. Once there is thorough understanding of the proposed projects, the team then has the job of selecting those that should receive funding.

The round one ranking can be revealed now to show the first round priority of selection. If there are more funds requested than available, then a round two process can be used to select the highest priority projects. If resolution cannot be accomplished within the ceiling development project budgeted amount, then sometimes the level of funding for certain projects must be negotiated and reduced. Lower priority project champions may negotiate some reduced level of introduction or continued funding rather than risk having no funding at all. It is a healthy environment for project champions to be authorized, prepared, and capable of real-time funding negotiations. This exercise can make all the difference in the ability of an organization to create and/or continue progress on certain proposed development projects. An iteration process may be necessary moving into round three (and further). Key deliberations are vital for selecting the strongest and most worthy projects at the respective levels of funding to maximize the progress for the organization toward the vision. Deliberations for project selection can be spirited, but this is a most important work for an effective organization.

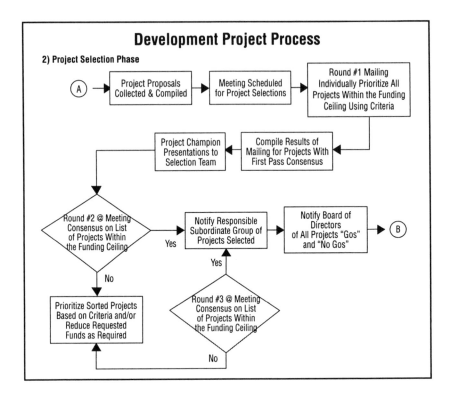

Development Project Selection Matrix

A special challenge for any development project selection team is to determine which are the best development projects to receive limited development funding. The short answer suggests the best projects are ones that are most compatible with—and provide the greatest progress toward—the vision of the organization. The proposed development projects may or may not be of high revenue-generating capability and they may be either long term or short term. Whatever the revenue capability or length of the project, it is imperative that the projects selected provide some special product or service that benefits current or new members and is in alignment with the organizational vision and ENDs.

It is helpful, therefore, to compare all the development project options against criteria for selection, as shown in the figure. All options should be evaluated against a common set of parameters that can be called criteria. As shown in the figure, the criteria should include all the ENDs of the organization as well as any other parameters that are significant to the progress of the organization, such as revenue potential, customer satisfaction, achievability or practicality, and the negative aspects, if this project is not selected for implementation. By aligning all the proposed development projects against the same selection criteria, it is possible to determine which projects are the strongest. Although opinions will vary among selection team members, this matrix analysis tool can yield a composite priority ranking of development projects and can give some common ground to help make the consensus process flow more naturally.

Development Project Selection Matrix

	Development Project Options				
	Project #1	Project #2	Project #3	Project #4	Etc.
End #1					
End #2					
End #3					
End #n					
Revenue Potential					
Customer Satisfaction					
Plan Achievability					
Negative Impact					
Total					

Priority of Importance Scale: 3 = High   2= Medium   1 = Low
(Projects with the highest total points are highest relative importance.)

Project Implementation Phase

Once the projects have been selected and the responsible subordinate groups have been notified, work should begin on the milestones targeted for completion during the coming year. The board of directors may wish to include some monitoring scheme to provide assurances that progress is on schedule and resulting in the gains that were anticipated.

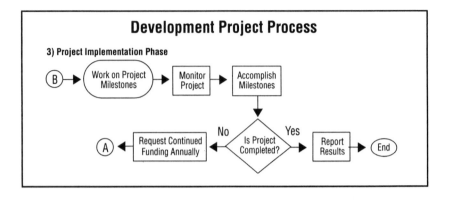

As the milestones are reached, the organization should begin to reap vital benefits resulting from progress toward special development projects. If projects involve multiyear funding, they need to be submitted annually to request continued funding. This approach causes all proposed development projects, whether new or continuing, to be sifted through the sieve of priority. This approach forces all funded projects to achieve the most annual gains possible for progress toward the vision—or risk no future funding. An effective board needs to have assurances that the development funds are (1) properly set aside and committed and (2) a process is in place to annually effectively allocate funds to the most deserving development projects.

Chapter 16

Foundations

Foundation Definition

Foundations can be an excellent segment of the provisions cog of the engineered organizational model. An effective board should be visionary and take time to understand the value of a foundation to support the long-term aims of the organization. A foundation can be defined as a subordinate, not-for-profit organization established to manage a permanent fund for charitable, educational, religious, or other benevolent purpose. The purpose of a foundation is to provide monetary and financial grants (rather than developed products or services from the organization) to forward the causes for which the foundation was established. A foundation usually is established with its own set of bylaws to define the nonprofit charter with a clear statement of purpose and rules of continuity related to the funds and management of the organization. Foundations usually are incorporated and established with a tax-exemption status. Because a foundation is a separate entity, it is managed by an separate body of directors or trustees. The principles of good governance are directly applicable to the processes of establishing, leading, and guiding foundations.

Foundation Board of Trustees

Larger organizations that have become established and effective at what they do are natural candidates for further expansion by creating a new arm of their organization called a foundation board. This board of trustees can be created to facilitate monetary contributions to provide an additional source of financial strength beyond those funds normally available to support the vision and purpose of the parent organization.

A sound financial policy related to foundation funds should be established. This policy is needed to ensure the foundation maintains ongoing fiscal stability and viability. A foundation should have on hand or should acquire the financial competency to meet the obligations of ongoing funding for special program commitments. Under the direction of the board of trustees, fund raising should be a key part of the activity of the foundation. Fund raising may come from several areas, including individuals, government agencies, and/or other public or private corporation foundations.

Relationship to Corporate Foundations

Most major multinational companies have established corporate foundations to provide grants to community service organizations. Typically, a corporate officer or team of officers is placed in charge of the corporate foundation and has the role of determining and designating the desired annual charitable contributions for the corporation. Corporation foundation managers look for several key indicators to determine viability of contributions to outside sources, including not-for-profit charitable foundations. Indicators often focus on the value and pertinence of new and past programs and how responsible the board of trustees is. The following are typical questions:

- What is the structure of the board of trustees?
- How involved are the members of the board?
- What past program successes have been shown?
- What new pertinent programs are in need of funding?

Assuming your organization can demonstrate the worthiness of the new and pertinent programs, the true value of an effective foundation board lies in proving involvement. One way to do that is through strong trustee personal financial involvement.

Trustee Financial Involvement

The foundation board should have a focused purpose for a common good to support the vision of the organization. For the foundation to be successful at receiving and significantly expanding corporate and individual giving, it is important that board members show personal support by making a donation themselves to the foundation. The amount of this board member giving often is irrelevant, but the fact that some participation has occurred can be quite meaningful. For the fund raising personnel to be able to show a significant board member financial involvement (ideally 100 percent participation by the board members) shows a powerful interest and involvement in the purpose for which the foundation was created. Personal involvement of the board demonstrates that the board is truly interested, involved, and in charge for the future.

Expectations for the members of the board should be created early in their terms of office to make this a routine part of establishing commitment to the purposes of the organization.

In the example shown, for year number 2, the total dollars given by the trustees was comparatively large, but the number of trustees participating was comparatively low. This shows a less-

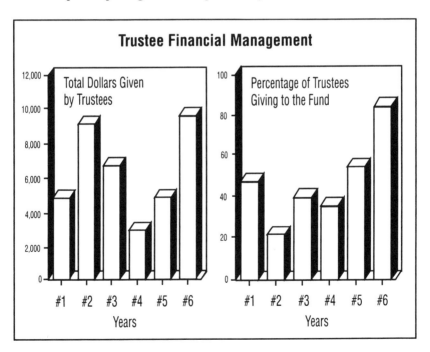

than-desirable indication of perhaps a lack of unity of purpose. Although motives may have been pure, one trustee may have made a single large donation while the other members were unwilling to support the views of that trustee and chose not to participate with their own resources. For year number 6, the total dollars given was not only relatively large, but the number of trustees involved was high as well. For this year, there is a much better indication of unity, commitment, and support of the overall purpose. This visible unity and commitment of the trustees and the board members can make the job of fund raising much more effective.

Responsibilities of the Foundation Board of Trustees

The responsibilities of the board of trustees for a foundation include overall credible financial management. This board should work to create and establish missions statements for the foundation that support the overall vision and direction of the parent organization. In addition, the board must organize and manage fund raising for the foundation. They need to seek out charitable gifts, contributions, and bequests to the foundation, including special earmarked funds that meet the intent of the vision. These funds need to be established with sufficient latitude to give long-term flexibility as required. They also must require special ongoing provisions to maintain applicability to the purpose of the organization.

Another responsibility of the board is to research and select special uses for foundation funds. These funds must be distributed in a way to support the missions determined by the board. The foundation board must manage for the safety of undistributed foundation funds. This means the basic fund balances must be invested sufficiently to cause sustaining growth, especially involving long-term scholarship and memorial funds. The board must monitor results through reports, audits, statements, and various forms of analyses using accepted auditing practices. The board should be sure that appropriate financial statements are created and maintained. It is a good idea to use independent auditing services annually to provide assurance of fiscal correctness.

There are two negative aspects of foundation board member performance that should be kept in mind and avoided at all costs. The first relates to confidentiality—an aspect of the board member responsibility that sometimes is taken for granted but can cause many problems if taken lightly. It is important for the board to maintain donor anonymity as requested by special contributing persons or organizations. Any disruption in this area can cause great problems in the future and it is impossible to undo once the "lid is off."

The second negative relates to tax status. Board members absolutely must refrain from any activity that would jeopardize the federal income tax exemption status of the organization. For example, many foundations are structured under a special tax-exemption status. An important category of tax-exempt status for an organization is found in Internal Revenue Code 501(c)(3). This states that representatives of the organization are prohibited from lobbying activities and that no personal financial benefit may be provided to individual members, officers, or members of the board. The board should take responsibility to ensure operations within these tax-related limitations.

A positive responsibility of the board relates to communication. It is important that the board be effective at descriptive communication of the work of the foundation to the extent that maximizes the overall purpose. One helpful form of communication is in the professionalism of published financial statements, along with visible progress of the programs being supported by the foundation. The foundation should publish an annual report showing the financial condition, activities being supported, and lists of funds and where they were distributed. This annual report should be made available for inspection by the membership, donors, and recipients.

Trustee—Crucial Communication Linkage

Private and corporation foundation managers typically are not anxious to subsidize deficits, but they can become very excited about funding new programs that fulfill mutual needs of the community, especially if they command interest in a greater good. Trustees do not have to be fund raisers themselves, but often they can be a crucial communication link to help set up meetings to link the fund raiser personnel to the private or corporation foundation managers. The contacts of trustees can help initial fundraising efforts as well as the follow-up communication about program progress. A good foundation can be synergistically beneficial to all concerned and can be part of the pride and power of an effective board.

Bibliography

Albrecht, Karl. *The Only Thing That Matters,* HarperCollins Publishers, Inc., 1992.

Byham, William C. "Targeted Selection," Development Dimensions Int'l, 1977.

Carver, John C. *Boards That Make a Difference,* Jossey-Bass, 1991.

Duca, Diane J. *Nonprofit Boards: A Practical Guide to Roles, Responsibilities, and Performance,* Onyx Press, 1986.

Graham, John W., and Wendy C. Havlick. *Mission Statements—A Guide to the Corporate and Nonprofit Sectors,* Garland Publishing, Inc., 1994.

Grove, Andrew S. *High Output Management,* Random House, Inc., New York, 1983.

Katzenbach, Jon R., and Douglas K. Smith. *The Wisdom of Teams,* Harvard Business School Press, 1993.

Maslow, Abraham H. *Motivation and Personality,* Harper & Row, 1954.

Nader, Ralph. *Taming the Giant Corporation,* W.W. Norton & Company, Inc., 1976.

Pfeiffer & Company, *Rules for Reaching Consensus,* 1994.

Richards, R. R. "Leadership: Leader to Leader," *Leadership,* American Society of Association Executives, 1995.

SAE International. *"Governance Policy Manual,"* 1995.

Senge, Peter M. *The Fifth Discipline—The Art & Practice of the Learning Organization,* Doubleday, 1990.

Tecker, Glenn, and Marybeth Fidler. *Successful Association Leadership,* Foundation of American Society of Association Executives, 1993.

Waldo, Charles N. *A Working Guide for Directors of Not-for-Profit Organizations,* Greenwood Press, 1986.

Wolf, Thomas. *The Nonprofit Organization: An Operating Manual,* Prentice-Hall, 1984.

Glossary

Actions—Activities that are performed to move the organization toward achieving missions, ends, and the vision. These may be part of the strategic plan. Note: This is nonboard work (see *Tasks*).

Board of Directors—The highest ranking leadership group and governing body of the organization. Has ultimate authority and responsibility for the organization. Sometimes called Board of Trustees or the Board.

Chair of the Board—Leader of the board and facilitator of governance practices, either established consciously by the board or based on prevailing traditions.

Cogs of the Organization—See *Engineered Organizational Model.*

Customer—Anyone who has needs or expectations, whether internal or external to the organization.

Chief Staff Officer—The top staff person who reports to the board of directors. Sometimes called Executive Vice President, Managing Director, Executive Secretary, etc.

Consensus—A form of agreement. Consensus occurs when at least 70 percent agree they like and support the proposal as presented and the other 30 percent say they wouldn't write it or present it just that way, but they, too, will support it. One hundred percent will support the proposal. Used instead of the voting process. Key question from Chair: "Can we all support this?"

Development Project—A funded or financially subsidized expansion or trial entrance into a product, process, or service that investigates, fosters, and demonstrates the feasibility of progress toward the vision with viable and consequential membership benefits for current and/or new members.

Empowerment—A cultural attitude of employees and members who are efficiently and effectively working to cause win-win outcomes for their customers and the organization.

ENDs Policies—These policies contain statements of vision and long-range direction for the organization. Answers any portion or all of the questions: what good (products, impacts, benefits, or outcomes), for whom (expected recipients), at what cost (acceptable costs for clarification). Updated and reexplored at least annually, they usually occur in sets subordinate to a vision statement. Defines and clarifies detail of the organizational vision.

Engineered Organizational Model—A mechanical visualization of an organizational model developed to define the relationships that leverage leadership to the benefit of the whole organization through three vital elements of policy (governance model), people, and provisions. The model is labeled as cogs of the organization and is used to reengineer and continuously improve the efficiency and effectiveness of the organization.

Fourth-Quadrant Thinking—Cultural thinking of an individual, team, board, or organization that embodies combined leader and manager characteristics. Practical visionaries, thinking long term and acting short term.

Governance Model—The part of the engineered organizational model that provides answers to the fundamental leadership issues of vision, values, authority, and roles. Includes the board's shared expressions of values through limitations, relationship, and governance process policies. See *Cogs of the Organization.*

Governance Process Policies—Policies that document the philosophy and style of governance used by the board. They define how the organization is governed. They also define officer roles and responsibilities and board job products.

Job Products—Desired outcomes, expectations, and results, including products, services, processes, or functional requirements that support the purpose of the organization.

Leader—One who helps establish direction, aligns people, motivates and inspires others, and produces change.

Leadership—The dynamic process used by the group to produce change toward the vision.

Limitations Policies—These policies, written in negative language, define the limits and boundaries of acceptable means-related activity within which subordinate groups and staff must operate. All processes, operations, methods, and activities must be within these parameters.

Manager—One who does planning and budgeting, organizes, and controls. One who is good at problem solving and producing order.

Market Directed—An organizational culture with a balance of power, in which who makes the decision, whether member or staff, is not nearly as important as the quality of the decision that is knowledge-based to benefit all stakeholders.

Means—Anything contrasted to ends. Deals with hows.

Member—Anyone who is a part of the organization as defined by the rules of the organization.

Member Driven—An organization where member officers are at the root of all major decisions. See *Staff Driven* and *Market Directed.*

Missions—Means statements. Answers "what we want to do." Sometimes confused with vision statements. Missions can be part of the strategic plan included with more specific goals and action details.

Objectives—A confusing term that has been applied to all kinds of subjects, including ends and means. "Objectives" is a term to avoid and is intentionally not used in the governance model concept.

People Cog—One of three cogs of the engineered organizational model. Human resources of the organization.

Policy—Any utterance of the board written for providing definition, understanding, and communication for the benefit of the organization. Policy can be captured only within the four categories of policy described in the governance model.

Policy Cog—One of three cogs of the engineered organizational model. Includes the governance model that can be used to increase effectiveness of the organization.

Policy Manual—A manual that contains all the written policies of the board grouped into the four segments of vision/ENDs, governance process, relationships, and limitations.

Provisions Cog—One of three cogs of the engineered organizational model. Financial resources of the organization.

Purpose—The underlying reason the organization exists. Usually documented in bylaws—the highest in the hierarchy of documents.

Relationship Policies—These policies describe the passing of power throughout the organization. They give delegation of authority and clarify roles, expectations, and job products for subordinate groups and the chief staff officer.

Rubber Stamp Syndrome—A board attitude stemming from seemingly too much to do so they must take blind action just to keep moving. This results from regular bogged down board agendas that are crammed with too many detailed items and issues, most of which could be delegated.

Scoreboard—Tool to track the progress of the board for completing governance tasks.

Staff Driven—An organization where staff are at the root of all major decisions. See *Member Driven* and *Market Directed*.

Strategic Plan—An important tool that documents the missions, activities, goals, and actions for addressing the critical issues. Can be used to ensure and monitor progress toward the vision. This plan must be created and owned by the subordinate organization because it is not a job product of the board.

Subordinate Groups—Any operating group, committee, or board that reports to the board of directors or an intermediary operating group, committee, or board.

Tasks—Work of the board. Activities of doing the leading, managing, and particularly governing of the organization. See *Actions*.

Teams—A small number of people with complementary skills who are committed to a common purpose, performance goals, and approach for which they hold themselves mutually accountable.

Top-Tier Monitoring—Active focus on key organizational progress toward the vision.

Vision—A macro view of the future and direction for the organization targeted five to ten years ahead. Answers any portion or all of the questions: what good, for whom, at what cost.

Visioning—The picturing of a positive, upward, outward, and future-oriented state. Begins with imagination. Creative thinking brought to the surface and employed to ensure original, innovative, yet realistic, input for successful visioning or picturing the new and desired future state.

Determine Visions
Versus Missions

This exercise will help you craft your own vision and mission statements. By evaluating the various vision and mission statements that follow, you'll begin to learn the principles involved in creating vision and mission statements. Some of the statements that follow are vision statements, and some are mission statements.

You may wish to review the chapter on vision and ENDs (Chapter 3) before you begin. This exercise will help you practice applying ENDS and MEANS thinking to visions and missions. The answers are shown at the end.

Vision vs. Mission Questions

1. **Rubbermaid Incorporated:** Be the leading world-class producer of best value, brand-name, primarily plastic products for the consumer, commercial, agricultural, and industrial markets which are responsive to significant trends. Vision or Mission?

2. **Mary Kay Cosmetics, Inc.:** To manufacture, distribute, and market personal care products through our independent sales force. To provide our sales force an unparalleled opportunity for financial independence, career achievement, and personal fulfillment. To achieve total customer satisfaction worldwide by focusing on quality, value, convenience, and personal service. Vision or Mission?

3. **J. C. Penny:** To sell merchandise and services to consumers at a profit, primarily but not exclusively in the United States, in a manner that is consistent with our corporate ethics and responsibilities. Vision or Mission?

4. **Steelcase, Inc.:** Be the best office environment company in the world. Provide customers with worldwide office environment products, services, and information that fully satisfy their requirements. Vision or Mission?

5. **Alabama Electric Cooperative, Inc.:** An economical and reliable power supply for our members through purchase, generation, and transmission of electric energy. Vision or Mission?

6. **Levi Strauss:** To sustain profitable and responsible commercial success by marketing jeans and selected casual apparel under the Levi's brand. Vision or Mission?

7. **American Management Association:** Educational forums worldwide where members and their colleagues learn superior, practical business skills and explore best practices of world-class organizations through interaction with each other and expert faculty practitioners. Vision or Mission?

8. **American Red Cross:** A humanitarian organization, led by volunteers, providing relief to victims of disasters and helping people prevent, prepare for, and respond to emergencies. Vision or Mission?

9. **Southwest Airlines Co.:** To provide the highest quality of Customer Service delivered with a sense of warmth, friendliness, individual pride and Company spirit. Vision or Mission?

10. **Anacomp, Inc.:** Innovative, cost-saving products, services, and solutions to meet our clients' information storage and retrieval needs today, tomorrow, and into the 21st century. Vision or Mission?

11. **ARCO Chemical Company:** Chemicals, related products, and services that enhances value for our stockholders, customers, employees, and to the public. Vision or Mission?

12. **Du Pont:** Constantly evolving and continually searching for new and better ways to use our human, technological, and financial resources to improve the quality of life of people around the world. Vision or Mission?

13. **Avon Products, Inc.:** The company that best understands and satisfies the product, service, and self-fulfillment needs of women globally. Vision or Mission?

14. **Browning-Ferris Industries:** The highest quality waste collection, transportation, processing, disposal, and related services to both public and private customers worldwide. Vision or Mission?

15. **Christian Broadcasting Network, Inc.:** To prepare the United States of America, the nations of the Middle East, the Far East, South America, and other nations of the world for the coming of Jesus Christ and the establishment of the kingdom of God on earth. Vision or Mission?

16. **Federal Express Corp.:** To produce outstanding financial returns by providing totally reliable, competitively superior global air-ground transportation of high-priority goods and documents that require rapid, time certain delivery. Vision or Mission?

17. **Ocean Spray Cranberries, Inc.:** Ocean Spray Quality, Everywhere. Quality means that Ocean Spray people will establish and live a quality level so high that it becomes the "gold standard." This means quality is not only what we do, but how we do it. Everywhere means that Ocean Spray beverage products will be available wherever and whenever the consumer has a need. Vision or Mission?

18. **Motorola, Inc.:** In each of our chosen arenas of the electronics industry, we plan to grow rapidly by providing our worldwide customers what they want, when they want it, with Six Sigma quality and best-in-class cycle time, as we strive to achieve our stated goals of increased global market share, best-in-class people, products, marketing, manufacturing, technology and service, and superior financial results. Vision or Mission?

19. **United States Air Force:** The world's most respected air and space force…global power and reach for America. Vision or Mission?

Answer

1. **Vision.** Deals with external things of what good (world-class producer...primarily plastic products) and for whom (the customer).

2. **Mission.** The focus is on internal things (manufacture, distribute, and market). It uses verbs (manufacture, provide, achieve, etc.).

3. **Mission.** The main focus is on internal things (sell, profit, in a manner...). Also starts with a verb (sell) implying action rather than a description of a future state.

4. **Vision.** Deals with external things of what good (world's best office environment products) and for whom (customers).

5. **Vision.** Deals with external things of what good (economical and reliable power supply) and for whom (our members).

6. **Mission.** The main focus is on internal things (profit, commercial success, and marketing). Also starts with a verb (sustain) implying action rather than description of a future state.

7. **Vision.** Deals with external things of what good (educational forums worldwide) and for whom (members).

8. **Vision.** Deals with external things of what good (a humanitarian organization) and for whom (to victims of disasters).

9. **Mission.** The main focus is on internal things (quality customer service) and hows (warmth, friendliness, etc.). Also starts with a verb (to provide).

10. **Vision.** Deals with external things of what good (innovative, cost-saving products, services, and solutions) and for whom (our clients).

11. **Vision.** Deals with external things of what good (chemicals, related products, and services) and for whom (our stockholders, customers, employees, and the public).

12. **Mission.** The main focus is on internal things (constantly evolving and continually searching for new and better ways). Also uses verbs (evolving, searching) implying action rather than description of a future state.

13. **Vision.** Deals with external things of what good (the company that best understands…and for whom (women).

14. **Vision.** Deals with external things of what good (highest quality waste services) and for whom (public and private customers worldwide).

15. **Mission.** The main focus is on action things for various places (U.S., Middle East, etc.). Starts with a verb (to prepare) implying action rather than description of a future state.

16. **Mission.** The main focus is on internal things (outstanding financial returns). Also starts with a verb (produce) implying action rather than description of a future state.

17. **Vision.** Deals with external things of what good (quality everywhere) and for whom (the consumer).

18. **Mission.** The main focus is on internal things (outstanding financial returns). Also uses verbs (grow, strive, achieve) implying action rather than description of a future state.

19. **Vision.** Deals with external things of what good (global power) and for whom (America).

Determine ENDs Versus Means

What type of policy is involved here? Where could I quickly find this type of board policy? These questions often are asked. This exercise reviews the process, provides hypothetical scenarios, and asks you to determine what type of policy is involved according to the governance model. Your answers should not be based on whether or not you just believe it should be board policy somewhere or whether it should be in the board agenda. Your answer should be based on the governance model and appropriate board policy type.

The following questions will help you to evaluate your own understanding of governance and board policy. These questions also can serve as a sample starter set for helping to structure a governance quiz for orientation at scheduled training sessions for incoming board members or for ongoing refreshers for the whole board.

ENDs Versus Means Questions

1. **Is the following an ENDs or a Means?**
   Consensus will be sought for decisions put before the board. All board members will have an opportunity to present their views.
2. **Is the following an ENDs or a Means?**
   A worldwide network of technically informed people for our customers.

3. **Is the following an ENDs or a Means?**

   The board will plan an annual agenda at its Organizing Session. The agenda will include evaluating and developing new ENDs policies, monitoring performance, revisiting means policies, implementing the board's governance process, and reviewing incidental information. A three-day Long-Range Planning Meeting will be held annually and will be extensively devoted to ENDs work.

4. **Is the following a Governance Process or an ENDs?**

   The president chairs the board meetings with all the commonly accepted power of that position.

5. **Is the following an ENDs or a Means?**

   A better natural environment for the benefit of future generations.

6. **Is the following an ENDs or a Means?**

   Each subordinate group may establish rules for its operation. Significant changes to the rules should be communicated to the board of directors.

7. **Is the following an ENDs or a Means?**

   Monitoring subordinate group performance is synonymous with monitoring organizational performance against applicable board policies. Any evaluation of performance, formal or informal, may be derived only from these monitoring data.

8. **Is the following a Relationship or a Limitation?**

   The executive vice president's job product includes favorable perception of the organization and public relations among key leaders in industry, government, and academia.

9. **Is the following an ENDs or a Limitation?**

   The chief staff officer may not cause or allow comingling of Foundation finances with the operating accounting and finances.

10. **Is the following an ENDs or a Limitation?**

    Differentiated specialty machinery of recognized superior value to worldwide customers.

11. **Is the following an ENDs or a Limitation?**
    Subordinate groups shall not exclude any qualified professional willing to participate within the organizational policies.
12. **Is the following a Governance Process or Relationship Policy?**
    The role of the treasurer is to review financial statements, confirm budgets, develop fiscal policies, and review business plans.

ENDs Versus Means Responses

1. This is a **means** (governance process—governing style policy) because it deals with an element of the desired governing style of the board and this answers the question "how?" (consensus). A good tip in identifying means is that it usually includes a verb.
2. This is an **END** (ENDs policy) because it answers the questions "what good?" (a network for technically informed people) and "for whom?" (worldwide customers).
3. This is a **means** (governance process policy) because it deals with how the board will do its job (plan an annual agenda and organize a three-day long-range planning meeting).
4. This is a **governance process** (role of the president) because it deals with an element of the president's role—means policy.
5. This is an **END** because it answers the questions "what good?" (a better natural environment) and "for whom?" (future generations).
6. This is a **means** (governance process policy) because it deals with how the subordinate groups of boards and committees will do their job (may establish their own rules).
7. This is a **means** because it deals with how the board will monitor performance. It is a relationship policy because it describes one aspect of the board's relationship with subordinate groups.
8. This is a **relationship** policy, one of the three types of means policies, because it describes the board's delegation of

responsibility to the executive vice president (favorable public relations). This is more specifically a relationships—chief staff officer job products—policy.

9. This is a **limitation** policy because it is written in negative language and puts a limitation on how the chief staff officer will do the job (not comingle finances).

10. This is an **ENDs** policy because it answers the questions "what good?" (machinery) and "for whom?" (worldwide customers).

11. This is a **limitation** policy because it's written as a negative statement and limits how subordinate groups will do their job (not limit participation of qualified professional).

12. This is a **governance process** policy because it deals with the role of an officer of the organization.

Determine Board Business

Is this board business? Is board approval required? These are frequently asked questions. This exercise reviews the process, provides hypothetical scenarios, and gives you the opportunity to determine whether these examples are board business or not according to the governance model. Your answers should not be based on traditional thinking as to whether or not it should be board business. Your responses should be based on the governance model, and you should be able to prove your response using the definitions of the governance model.

Reviewing the following questions will help you evaluate your understanding of governance and board policy. These questions also can help you develop your own set of questions to structure a governance quiz for orientation at scheduled training sessions before a board meeting.

Governance Questions

1. A board member says the vision of the organization is confusing and needs to clarified. Is this board business?
2. Some 8,000 members of the Antique Covered Wagon Association decide to move their activities to our organization, and they want to establish a new board or major committee to serve their needs. Is this board business?
3. CNN calls the chair of one of the subordinate committees to schedule a televised interview to publicize why and how the organization is doing so well. The committee chair has agreed to the interview. Is this board business?

4. Staff create a policy to require every staff member to contribute to United Way. Is this board business?

5. The staff policy handbook is modified—caning will be the punishment for extending coffee breaks. Is this board business?

6. The Finance Committee decides to restructure itself into three separate committees reporting to the board. Is this board business?

7. A board member proposes an agenda item to eliminate the security officer at the headquarters office. Is this board business?

8. A board member decides that governance terms, such as ENDs, relationships, and limitations, are too confusing and should be modified. Is this board business?

9. More than 50 members in Czechoslovakia decide they want to form a new affiliate group called the Czech Affiliate. Is this board business?

10. A group of members of the organization has strong feelings that the direction of the organization should be changed to encompass a whole new segment for the future. Is this board business?

Governance Question Responses

1. Yes. Board policy includes the vision statements of the organization. If the vision statement is deemed unclear by a board member, it is important to clarify it, whether through revised written policy or in personal clarification to the board member.

2. Yes. Board policy indicates the board is responsible for establishing operating boards and permanent committees that report to it.

3. Yes. Board policy prohibits members to speak publicly on behalf of the organization. Further, the policy on the president's role indicates only the president can speak on behalf of the organization.

4. **No.** Board policy authorizes staff to establish staff policies, make decisions, and take action, as long as they are consistent with a reasonable interpretation of all board policies.

5. **Yes.** Board policy says the chief staff officer may not cause or allow staff to be treated counter to accepted practices of human rights.

6. **Yes.** Board policy indicates the board is responsible for establishing committees that report to the board. The Finance Committee's input should be considered as a recommendation to the board as a proposed policy modification to the relationships policy.

7. **No.** Security and safety of assets is a job product of the chief staff officer. This subject is meddling in the business of the chief staff officer.

8. **Yes.** The board's governance process policy describes the board's policy language. Changing the terms, therefore, would be board business.

9. **Yes.** Board policy states affiliates are defined in relationships policy, and this is board business.

10. **Yes.** It is the job product of the board to define, document, and lead toward the stated vision and direction for the organization. If there is confusion or change here, then it is board business.

Policy Manual Example

Policy of the Board of Directors

The following are sample reference pages for a policy manual based on the governance model. Four types of sample policies are shown, including ENDs, governance process, relationships, and limitations. These policies are intended to be generic and can serve as input for a representative beginning set of policies. These can provide a "jump start" to help get the cogs of your organization turning with leveraged leadership.

Policy Type: ENDS
Title: VISION

The vision of the organization is: _____

_____

The ENDs of the organization are:

1. _____

_____

2. _____

_____

3. _____

_____

etc.

Policy Type: GOVERNANCE PROCESS

Title: THE BOARD'S GOVERNANCE PROCESS

The form of governance to be used by the Board of Directors will be characterized by documentation and communication of the Board's shared expressions of values through policies in the four major segments of ENDs, Governance Process, Relationships, and Limitations. These policies will provide leadership responses to fundamental issues of vision, values, authority, and roles.

1.   Board policies on ENDs: These will state "what good" (products, impacts, benefits, or outcomes), "for whom" (expected recipient), and at "what cost" (acceptable costs for clarification to the organization), updated and reexplored at least annually.

2.   Board policies on GOVERNANCE PROCESS: These will state the philosophy and methods of the Board of Directors' own operations, including Board job products, governing style, Board member and officer roles and responsibilities, use of Board subteams, bylaw interpretation as needed, and subordinate group appointment process.

3.   Board policies on RELATIONSHIPS: These will establish subordinate groups (composition, scope/authority, and job products) and state the nature of delegation to staff and Chief Staff Officer job products.

4.   Board policies on LIMITATIONS: These will state subordinate group actions, the Chief Staff Officer and staff actions that would be unacceptable to the Board.

5.   A two-step process will be used to establish or amend policies.

5.1 1st action—Agreement on a concept or draft of a new or amended policy as discussed at a regular meeting of the Board.

5.2 2nd action—Adoption of the proposed new or amended policy at a following regular meeting of the Board, with a copy of the proposed policy mailed to each member of the Board at least 10 days before the meeting at which action is to be taken. The new or amended policy will take affect immediately on its passage by the Board.

6.   ...etc.

Policy Type: GOVERNANCE PROCESS

Title: GOVERNING STYLE

The governing style of the Board of Directors will optimize diversity, teamwork, proactivity, self-discipline, the long view, customer focus, win-win deliberation, full participation, and maximum empowerment of subordinate groups of the organization.

The governing style will be characterized in the following ways:
1.   Roles, responsibilities, and job products of the Board of Directors, subordinate groups and the Chief Staff Officer will be clearly differentiated to avoid overlap, gaps, and ambiguities.
2.   A continuous improvement process for governance will be observed, including regular monitoring and discussions of the Board's own performance, performance of officers, and performance of the established subordinate groups of the organization.
3.   Orientation and periodic redevelopment of Directors will be provided.
4.   Sufficient organization and agenda time allocation will be scheduled for addressing the right topics at meetings of the Board.
5.   Consensus decisions will be sought for issues put before the Board. Board members will be given opportunity to surface their views.
6.   Administrative support and assistance of the Board's Governance Process will be provided by the Secretary. The Secretary will:
    6.1 Be knowledgeable of the Governance Process and Policy Manual, provide information on existing Board policies, and implement changes to the Policy Manual as directed by the Board.
    6.2 Identify Board deliberations that are inconsistent or contrary to the Board's policies so corrective direction can be taken.
7.   ...etc.

Policy Type: GOVERNANCE PROCESS

Title: BOARD MEMBER RESPONSIBILITIES

The Board expects of itself unconflicted loyalty to the purpose of the organization. This commitment includes proper use of authority and appropriate
decorum in group and individual behavior when acting as Board members.
Board members will:

1. Support and defend policies adopted by the Board.
2. Promote a climate of mutual trust, respect, and teamwork.
3. Avoid personal conflicts or perceived conflicts of interest, including acting
as agents or representatives of other organizations.
4. Plan to attend 100% of the scheduled Board meetings.
5. Be diligent in preparing for meetings of the Board.
6. Support the President to run effective meetings.
7. Refrain from individuality influencing the organization except as explicitly
set forth in Board policy.
8. Plan the Board's annual agenda at its Organizing Session. The agenda will
include:
    * Evaluating and developing new ENDs policies,
    * Monitoring performance,
    * Revisiting MEANS policies,
    * Implementing the Board's Governance Process, and
    * Reviewing incidental information.
9. ...etc.

Policy Type: GOVERNANCE PROCESS

Title: JOB PRODUCTS OF THE BOARD

On behalf of the members, the Board of Directors is to provide strategic
direction and clear leadership. The job products of the Board are:

1. Written Board Policies—Written Board policies will be broadly stated with
sufficiently thorough layers to capture and communicate all relevant values for
the successful aim and conduct of the organization.
2. Assurance of Performance—The Board will monitor subordinate group and
Chief Staff Officer performance using appropriate information.
3. Leadership Linkage—A two-way communication will be maintained with
the member community for momentum building and ENDs clarification.
4. ...etc. (See Chapter 2 for ideas pertinent to your Board.)

Policy Type: GOVERNANCE PROCESS

Title: ROLE OF THE PRESIDENT

The role of the President is to ensure the integrity of the Board's process and be the primary representative of the Board of Directors.

1. The President is to ensure that the Board behaves consistent with its own policies and the bylaws.
    1.1 Meeting discussion content will be only on those issues that clearly belong to the Board according to Board policy.
    1.2 Deliberation will be timely, fair, orderly, and sufficiently thorough, but also efficient with time restrictions and kept to the point.
2. The President is authorized to make reasonable decisions about the interpretation of policy regarding the Board's own job.
    2.1 The President chairs Board meetings with all the commonly accepted power of that position.
    2.2 The President has no authority to make decisions beyond policies created by the Board. The President, therefore, has no authority to change the Board expectations for subordinate groups or for the Chief Staff Officer.
    2.3 The President is to appoint individuals to subordinate groups.
3. The President is the official spokesperson of the organization.
4. …etc.

Policy Type: GOVERNANCE PROCESS

Title: ROLE OF THE TREASURER AND ASSISTANT TREASURER

The role of the Treasurer and Assistant Treasurer (along with the Board's Finance Committee) is to review financial statements, develop fiscal policies, review business plans, and confirm budgets.

1. The Treasurer and Assistant Treasurer will support and defend policies adopted by the Board of Directors.
2. The Treasurer and Assistant Treasurer are authorized to co-sign (with staff) checks over $5,000, sign notes, and manage stock and other securities owned by the organization.
3. ...etc.

Policy Type: GOVERNANCE PROCESS

Title: BOARD SUBTEAMS

1. Composition: Board Subteams shall be formed by the Board of Directors on an ad hoc basis. Board Subteams shall consist of Board members only and no more than eight volunteers. The subteam leader will be appointed by the President or the Board.
2. Scope/Authority: Board Subteams shall prepare specific policy options and implications for Board consideration as charged by the Board. Actions by Board Subteams shall be limited to the development of alternatives, and all actions on behalf of the organization shall be taken only by the Board.
3. Job Products: Policy options and implications as charged by the Board.
4. ...etc.

Policy Type: GOVERNANCE PROCESS

Title: SUBORDINATE GROUPS—
APPOINTMENTS AND ORGANIZATION

The President, subject to the approval of the Board of Directors, shall appoint the members of the subordinate groups, including the chairperson and vice chairpersons of each.

1. Members of all subordinate groups shall be voting members.
2. Each subordinate group may establish rules for its operation.
3. All subordinate groups shall perform the duties assigned to them.
4. The President and the Secretary shall be ex officio members of all subordinate groups.
5. Proposed expenditures of funds by such subordinate groups that jeopardize meeting the annual Return on Equity target must have prior Board authorization.
6. The Board of Directors may at any time remove any or all members of any committee or board.
7. Vacancies on subordinate groups shall be filled by appointment by the President, subject to approval by the Board.
8. Chairpersons of each major subordinate group may attend meetings of the Board and take part in pertinent discussions.
9. ...etc.

Policy Type: GOVERNANCE PROCESS

Title: DELEGATION TO SUBORDINATE GROUPS

Subordinate Groups are accountable to the Board of Directors and are governed by policies established by the Board.

1. The job products determined and actually accomplished by subordinate groups must be true to the broader statements of policies established by the Board of Directors.
2. The MEANS employed (practices, activities, methods, ways of conducting business, circumstances of operating, or any other work or behavior) may not violate the LIMITATIONS.
3. Subordinate grups are authorized to use "any reasonable interpretation" of the language used in Board policies.
4. Subordinate groups are expected to work cooperatively with other subordinate groups and staff.
5. ...etc.

Policy Type: RELATIONSHIPS—MEMBER

Title: COMMUNICATION

Subordinate groups shall provide the Board of Directors information, counsel, and insights necessary for the Board to govern well, including:

1. Vision and long-range aspirations needed for the Board of Directors to develop overall ENDs.
2. Data regarding subordinate group performance against expectations stated in the ENDs and MEANs policies of the Board of Directors, including foreseeable changes needed in policies of the Board.
3. Significant changes in subordinate group rules and procedures.
4. ...etc.

Policy Type: RELATIONSHIPS—MEMBER

**Title: MONITORING SUBORDINATE
         GROUP PERFORMANCE**

Monitoring subordinate group performance is synonymous with monitoring organizational performance against applicable Board policies.

1. The purpose of monitoring is simply to determine the degree to which Board policies are being fulfilled. Monitoring will be as automatic as possible, using a minimum of Board time so that meetings can be used to create the future rather than to review the past.
2. Upon the choice of the Board, any policy can be monitored by any method at any time. For regular monitoring, however, each policy will be classified by the Board according to frequency and method and documented in Board policy.
3. In planning agenda monitoring reports to the Board of Directors, a high priority will be given to Board-level issues regarding programs, services, or activities that are considered to be in jeopardy.
4. ...etc.

Policy Type: RELATIONSHIPS—MEMBER

Title: SUBORDINATE GROUPS— COMPOSITION, SCOPE/ AUTHORITY, AND JOB PRODUCTS

1. Foundation Board of Trustees   (An Example Board)

   1.1 Composition: The Foundation Board of Trustees shall consist of not more than eleven or fewer than nine voting members. The members of this Board shall include the Treasurer, a member of the Board of Directors appointed annually for a one-year term, and at least six other voting members appointed for three-year terms, with at least one and no more than two appointment terms expiring each year. One of the members will be appointed each year to serve as chairperson. Upon completion of a full term on this board, a member shall not be eligible for a further term until one year has elapsed.
   1.2 Scope/Authority: Facilitate financial contributions from members and others to provide an additional source of income beyond those sources normally available to the organization. These resources will be used in support of the purpose and strategic plans.
   1.3 Job Products: Financial management of contributions and funds.

2. Compensation Committee   (An Example Permanent Committee)

   2.1 Composition: The Compensation Committee shall consist of the President (as chairperson), the immediate Past President, the President Nominee/Elect, the Treasurer, and the Assistant Treasurer.
   2.2 Scope/Authority: To evaluate the performance of the Chief Staff Officer and to establish an appropriate compensation level. A report should be provided in executive session of the Board.
   2.3 Job Product: A formal performance evaluation for the Chief Staff Officer and an annual compensation level.

3. Finance Committee   (An Example Permanent Committee)

   3.1 Composition: The Finance Committee shall consist of the Treasurer, the Assistant Treasurer, and eight appointed members. One of the appointed members shall be appointed to chair the Committee. Two members shall be appointed each year for a four-year term. Upon completion of a four-year term, such members shall not be eligible for reappointment until one year has elapsed.

continued on page 202

continued from page 201

3.2 Scope/Authority: To supervise the financial affairs of the organization. The Finance Committee reports to the Board of Directors by presenting a statement of the financial condition at each regular meeting of the Board of Directors. At the last Board meeting of each fiscal year, the Committee shall present a target return on equity and budget of anticipated income and expense for the next fiscal year.

The Committee is authorized, subject to LIMITATIONS Board policy, to buy and sell:
- securities, in compliance with investment policies,
- fixed assets, not included in capital budgets, with an annual aggregate cost of not more than 10% of the organization's total net worth at the beginning of each fiscal year, and
- other assets and property with an aggregate annual cost of not more than 10% of the organization's total net worth.

The Finance Committee has authority to incur debt not to exceed 25% of the organization's total net worth.

The Finance Committee has authority to approve loans or long-term capital resources to affiliates up to the limits established by the Board.

3.3 Job Products

The Finance Committee supervises:
- Financial affairs, including investments and loans,
- Annual budget,
- Annual target return-on-equity rate,
- Financial reports,
- ...etc.

Policy Type: RELATIONSHIPS—MEMBER

Title: INTERNATIONAL RELATIONS

International Relations (An Example International Policy)

The organization shall engage in international relationships that foster an attitude of cordial friendship, cooperation, information interchange, and a general open-door policy.

1. Qualified applications for membership are welcomed from any country.
2. Programs, services, and activities (such as meetings, sections, expositions, conferences, publications, etc.) located anywhere in the world shall be aimed at meeting customer needs and consistent with ENDs.
3. Exchange of information shall be encouraged wherever and whenever it is mutually beneficial to membership and the local member community.
    3.1 In countries with existing sister organizations, subordinate groups are encouraged to look for mutually beneficial cooperative programs, services, and activities to foster the achievement of stated ENDs.
    3.2 In order to satisfy member needs worldwide, subordinate groups may pursue individual activities on their own in other countries.
4. …etc.

Policy Type: RELATIONSHIPS—MEMBER

Title: DELEGATION TO THE CHIEF STAFF OFFICER

The Chief Staff Officer is accountable to the Board of Directors for the support of achieving ENDs within LIMITATIONS policies.

1. All Board authority delegated to staff is delegated through the Chief Staff Officer. As far as the Board is concerned, all staff authority and accountability is considered to be that of the Chief Staff Officer.
    1.1 The Chief Staff Officer is accountable only to the full Board of Directors, not to any one individual Board member.
    1.2 The Chief Staff Officer is authorized to establish staff policies, make decisions, take action, and develop activities as long as they are consistent with a reasonable interpretation of Board policies.
    1.3 The Chief Staff Officer shall be a regular employee of the organization employed by the Board of Directors and shall also carry the title of Secretary of the Board and General Manager of Headquarters Operations.
2. …etc.

Policy Type: RELATIONSHIPS—MEMBER

**Title: CHIEF STAFF OFFICER
JOB PRODUCTS**

The job products of the Chief Staff Officer are staff and system capability, including:

1. Capability to achieve ENDS of the organization, including:
   1.1 Competency, continuity, progression, and succession of staff with:
      1.1.1 Staff compensation and benefits consistent with the market for employee skills and experience.
      1.1.2 Staff treated in a manner consistent with human rights.
      1.1.3 Two staff persons fully informed about and capable of performing the Chief Staff Officer functions in case of unexpected loss.
   1.2 Accurate, concise, and timely information, counsel and processes for the work of the Board of Directors and subordinate groups.
   1.3 Implementation of annual goals that support the Board's ENDS.
2. Fiscal stability, viability, and competency, including:
   2.1 Product and service obligations to the membership.
   2.2 Achievement of the targeted annual return on equity.
3. Safety of assets and legal status, including:
   3.1 Proper security, protection, and risk management of assets.
   3.2 Avoidance of any activity that would put the tax status at risk.
   3.3 Immediate suspension of any activity beyond the LIMITATIONS boundaries by any subordinate group.
   3.4 Proper notice to those individuals or other organizations found to be misusing the organization's name or logo.
   3.5 Use of official stationery only by officers and the staff.
4. Accurate and timely information, including:
   4.1 Monitoring data on subordinate group performance, with the measures and frequency established by the Board.
   4.2 Monitoring data on Chief Staff Officer performance, with the measures and frequency established by the Board.
   4.3 Relevant trends, incidents and developments, significant decisions, threatened or actual legal jeopardy, and changes in assumptions on which Board of Directors or subordinate group policies have been based.
   4.4 Optional points of view, information, analysis, and counsel necessary for fully informed knowledge-based Board choices.
5. Favorable perception of the organization among key leaders of the membership community in industry, government, and academia.
6. Intra-organizational communications for and with the Board, subordinate groups, officers, staff, and the member community.
7. ...etc.

Policy Type: RELATIONSHIPS—MEMBER
Title: MONITORING CHIEF STAFF
OFFICER PERFORMANCE

Monitoring Chief Staff Officer performance is synonymous with monitoring organizational performance against applicable Board policies.

1.   The purpose of monitoring is simply to determine the degree to which Board policies are being fulfilled. Monitoring will be as automatic as possible, using a minimum of Board time so that meetings can be used to create the future rather than to review the past.
2.   Upon the choice of the Board, any policy can be monitored by any method at any time. For regular monitoring, however, each policy will be classified by the Board according to frequency and method.
3.   The annual formal performance evaluation will be an examination of the year's regular monitoring and be performed by the Compensation Committee.
4. ...etc.

Policy Type: LIMITATIONS—MEMBER
Title: GENERAL CONSTRAINT—
SUBORDINATE GROUPS

Subordinate Groups shall not cause or allow any practice, activity, decision, or organizational circumstance, that is either imprudent or in violation of law, or of commonly accepted business and professional ethics. Subordinate Groups shall not:

1.   Operate in disregard of the interests of the organization.
    1.1 Use or commit resources including staff time and resources that jeopardize meeting the annual Return-on-Equity target.
    1.2 Work within the scope of other subordinate groups or the Chief Staff Officer or speak for the organization in any way reserved for the Board of Directors or others whom the Board has empowered.
2.   Operate in disregard of standards of integrity.
    2.1 Allow commercialism, including the endorsement of products, patents, processes, services, individuals, or ideas, except as specifically authorized by the Board of Directors.
    2.2 Exclude any qualified professional willing to participate within policies.
    2.3 Operate secretively.
    2.4 Engage in activity or communication that knowingly can lead to or appear to result in a conflict of interest, including acceptance of financial or other goods or benefits that might influence actions or decisions.
3.   Use the official letterhead for general communications.
4.   ...etc.

Policy Type: LIMITATIONS—MEMBER

Title: GENERAL CONSTRAINT— CHIEF STAFF OFFICER

The Chief Staff Officer shall not allow or cause any action or decision in his/her area of supervision and control that is either imprudent, illegal, unethical, or detracts from the purpose. Accordingly, the Chief Staff Officer may not cause or allow:

1. Comingling of the Foundation finances with operating finances.
2. Use of restricted net worth increases for operations.
3. Staff activity, communication, or benefit that knowingly can lead to or appear to result in a conflict of interest, including acceptance of financial or other goods or benefits that might influence actions or decisions.
4. Disbursement of funds for member leader travel costs.
5. Improper staff action.
   5.1 Employee activities in the annual nominating process are limited to providing information requested by a delegate, an alternate, a member wishing to make an at-large nomination, or nominating committees.
   5.2 Formation by staff of ad hoc member groups without specific request or permission of volunteer groups.
   5.3 Operate secretively except for confidential personnel matters.
6. ...etc.

Policy Type: LIMITATIONS—MEMBER

Title: FINANCIAL CONSTRAINT

Members and staff shall work within the following financial boundaries for overall fiscal stability.

1. No Negative Net Earnings—Expenses shall not exceed income for the fiscal year.
2. No Use of Funds Deviating from Board Policy—No budgeting shall deviate appreciably from organizational priorities expressed in ENDs policies of the Board.
3. No Unacceptable Risk—Financial estimates should not be based upon other than conservative estimates, and financial conditions are not permitted that jeopardize the fiscal stability for effective and prudent operations.
4. No Intermingling of Funds—No one, whether member or staff, has the freedom to arbitrarily move funds from one account to another.
5. ...etc.

Board Member Inventory

Successful organizations for the future will be made up of leaders who are continually learning and improving governance. It is good practice to regularly determine the benchmark on governance so progress can be measured. This valuable benchmark then can be used to focus on areas for improvement and later evaluate the progress.

To establish this benchmark, the following questionnaire can be used. The purpose is to clarify the current levels of board member satisfaction for important areas of governance. The results can be summarized to display a relative scale of governance performance.

In completing the questionnaire, each respondent should take into account the results and impressions over the last two or three board meetings or the last six months of operations.

This board inventory outlines your personal assessment of the attitudes, approach, and culture of your board. The inventory contains thirty pairs of behavioral and cultural descriptions. Consider each of the pairs to represent opposite ends of a six-point continuum. The descriptions do not imply good or bad, but simply offer different ways of approaching things.

Directions: For each pair, circle the number on the scale shown that you believe best describes the current environment. The extremes (0 and 6) represent very definite patterns of behavior or expressions of culture, whereas the middle (3) represents no particular preference for either of the descriptions. Even though it may be difficult at times, be sure to circle a number on the scale for each of the pairs. Avoid the middle ratings whenever possible. The more candid and honest you are, the more useful this inventory will be.

Board Agendas

Board freely addresses any agenda subject.	0 1 2 3 4 5 6	Board addresses only what is predefined as Board business.
Board time is typically over 70% listening to reports.	0 1 2 3 4 5 6	Board time is typically over 70% on policy deliberations.
Proposals are submitted to the Board for authorization.	0 1 2 3 4 5 6	Board mostly develops its own issues and proposals.
Members unofficially earn speaking rights through seniority.	0 1 2 3 4 5 6	Most Board members contribute ideas on Board issues.
Board prefers to focus on "the issues."	0 1 2 3 4 5 6	Board takes time to plan its agenda and track progress.

Approach to Governance

Expectations about Board work come with experience.	0 1 2 3 4 5 6	Board has preestablished its role and job products.
Traditional meetings require very little training.	0 1 2 3 4 5 6	Board members receive governance orientation annually.
Areas of confusion are opportunities to solve problems.	0 1 2 3 4 5 6	Areas of confusion are opportunities to clarify Board policy.
Subordinate groups come to the Board for "approvals."	0 1 2 3 4 5 6	Subordinate groups are expected to make their own decisions.
The strategic plan is top priority so people know what to do.	0 1 2 3 4 5 6	A clear vision is priority and is revisited and updated regularly.

Ownership

Board issues regularly involve operating procedures.	0 1 2 3 4 5 6	Board leads with selected, brief, and broad policy statements.
Board feels ownership through its approvals and decisions.	0 1 2 3 4 5 6	Board feels ownership through setting organizational direction.
Board expects reports with data to "keep the pressure on."	0 1 2 3 4 5 6	Board monitors progress with developed top-level measures.
Key input to the Chief Staff Officer is through problems.	0 1 2 3 4 5 6	Key input to the CSO is through an annual performance review.
Board expects adherence to Board utterances.	0 1 2 3 4 5 6	Board can tolerate "reasonable interpretations" of policy.

Decision-Making

Motions are voted and the "majority rules."	0 1 2 3 4 5 6	Board uses the consensus process.
Decisions are typically made from predetermined options.	0 1 2 3 4 5 6	Decisions are win-win outcomes from teamwork and diversity.
Conflict is usually resolved by searching for compromise.	0 1 2 3 4 5 6	Conflict is usually resolved by searching for common ground.
Most decisions are based on knowledge of key leaders.	0 1 2 3 4 5 6	Most decisions are knowledge-based with customer input.
Accomplishments take priority over trust and respect.	0 1 2 3 4 5 6	Trust and respect take priority over tangible accomplishments.

Sense of Purpose

Senior Board members speak more than the Freshmen.	0 1 2 3 4 5 6	Full Board contributes to its role and responsibilities.
No work is too large or too small for the Board.	0 1 2 3 4 5 6	Board knows what is—and what is not—Board business.
Personal satisfaction comes with time and experience.	0 1 2 3 4 5 6	Entire Board expresses feeling accomplishment.
Improving weaknesses/seeking the predictable is the culture.	0 1 2 3 4 5 6	Enhancing strengths and managing change is the culture.
Board time mostly involves resolution of internal issues.	0 1 2 3 4 5 6	Board time is mainly about issues external to the organization.

Organizational Linking

When in disagreement, people say, "This is what I think."	0 1 2 3 4 5 6	When in disagreement, people highlight, "This is the vision."
Communications are aimed at those who need to know.	0 1 2 3 4 5 6	Communications are aimed for widespread issue awareness.
Subordinate groups and staff often seek Board input.	0 1 2 3 4 5 6	The organization exhibits many actions of empowerment.
Written responsibilities are mostly for Board input.	0 1 2 3 4 5 6	Written responsibilities are mostly for Board communication.
The Board/Staff relationship is more one of conflict.	0 1 2 3 4 5 6	The Board/Staff relationship is more one of cooperation.

Scoring of the Inventory

Assessment Scoring Instructions

1) Transfer your answer for each item to the spaces provided below.
2) Add the scores as indicated.
3) Add the individual scores to calculate the overall effectiveness score.

Board Agendas

Approach to
Governance

Ownership

Decision-Making

Sense of Purpose

Organizational
Linking

Total _____

Total _____

Total _____

Total _____

Total _____

Total _____

"Cog"
Total _____

"Cog"
Total _____

"Cog"
Total _____

Score _____
Overall Total

Policy   People   Provisions

The Engineered Organizational Model

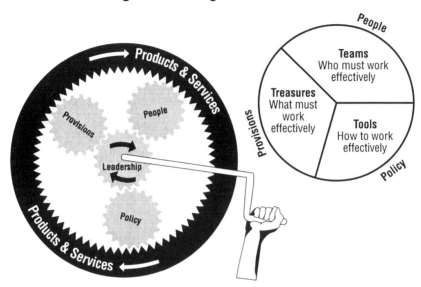

Cogs of the Organization

The engineered organizational model is shown as a machine and labeled as Cogs of the Organization. This overall organizational model has been developed to define and establish the fundamental relationships for leadership understanding. This model depicts the major components for a successful organization and visually describes and demonstrates how these pieces fit together for success.

The model begins with leadership as the core need of the organization. As shown, leadership can be leveraged to activate the three cogs of policy, people, and provisions into a powerful machine for creating products and services for the customers. "Leadership" is the beginning requirement and driver of all the three cogs.

The first cog is **Policy.** Policy includes the model for organizational governance. By default every organization has methods of governance—some good and some not so good. This describes organizational guidance methods, the purposes inherent in the organizational culture, and interprets "how we want to work together."

The next cog is **People.** People are who really make it happen and are most important for success. This element focuses ownership and organizational linking of the special people who contribute to the success. Additionally, relationships, training, and team thinking make up this cog that describes "who must work together."

The third cog is **Provisions.** Provisions is the cog of the organization that could be referred to as the combined personnel, financial, and asset resources that contribute to the organizational success. Decision-making processes, communication processes, and efficiencies in agendas and meetings contribute to efficiencies. The corporate treasures are "what we have to work with" to make progress for the future.

These cogs of policy, people, and provisions should each be strong. If one of these three cogs is weak or is missing, then the capability of the organization is lessened and the amount of products and services will be less than the potential. It takes all three of these components to leverage leadership and build for effectiveness.

Profile of the Inventory

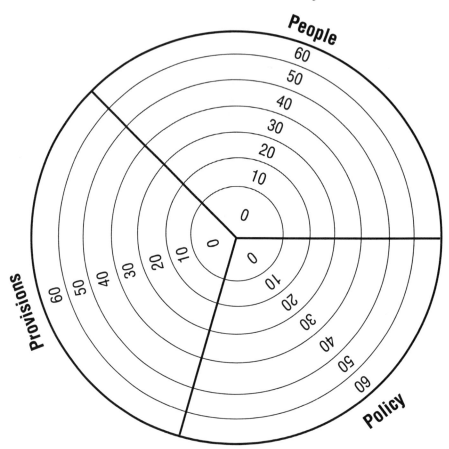

Inventory and Assessment

1) Circle your scores on the chart.

2) Connect your scores with straight lines to obtain a triangular shape.

3) Compare your results with the assessment profiles on page 213.

4) Build an effective Board for success!

Profiles and Patterns for Assessment

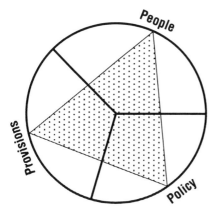

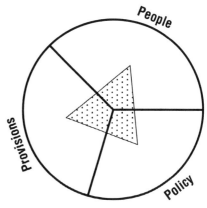

This profile reflects outstanding Board strengths in all the "cogs" of an organization. This profile represents an organization that is maximizing effectiveness in all areas. Keep up the good work. Your future is very bright!

This profile reflects Board weaknesses in all the "cogs" of an organization. This profile represents an organization that is not effective in any of the key areas. It will require considerable effort to build a new culture to gain in effectiveness. Your future is very questionable unless major thinking changes are quickly explored and implemented!

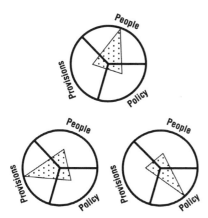

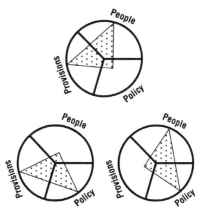

This profile reflects Board strengths in one of the three key "cogs" of the organization. You tend to rely on this strength to make progress. You need to expand development into both of the other areas to build a truly effective organization. Without some growth in the other two areas, future success will be diminished. Attention in the other two areas will pay big dividends for building an effective organization and help maximize progress to support the purpose.

This profile reflects Board strengths in two of the three key "cogs" of the organization. If weak in the "Policy" cog, you should investigate the application of the Governance Model to help gain in effectiveness. If weak in the "People" cog, you should implement team building. If weak in the "Provisions" cog, you should implement a total quality system to focus voice of the customer. Some adjustments will yield benefits and aid in your future success!

Overall Total Score Assessment

The following scales reflect both the overall score and the individual scores for the cogs of policy, people, and provisions. The larger values refer to the total overall score and the smaller values refer to the individual scores. You may wish to use this for your personal assessment of the current board environment, but the averaged scores of several or all members of the board can yield a very strong perception of the status.

180-151 Overall Score or 60-51 Individual Score

This score reflects outstanding strengths. You are part of an outstanding, progressive, performing, successful, and effective organization. You represent the model for the future. Your organization has learned how to maximize effectiveness in ways that foster growth. Keep up the good work. You are among the elite. Your future is very bright.

150-121 Overall Score or 50-41 Individual Score

This score shows you are working at gaining appropriate strengths. Much positive change has been introduced, but more consistency of application and implementation is needed to establish the true culture shift. You have learned much about maximizing effectiveness but a little more effort is needed to continue to shape the culture for progress.

120-91 Overall Score or 40-31 Individual Score

This score shows an encouraging approach for the future. More effort is needed to learn about and grow new thought patterns, develop new tools, implement teaming, and unleash the power within people. You are part of a growing organization that can continue to build for a bright future.

90-61 Overall Score or 30-21 Individual Score

This score shows the need for gaining appropriate strengths. Now is the time to sharpen the focus toward culture change. More attention is needed to ensure success in the future. More effort is required to implement a culture for success. The organization can continue for a while based on past momentum, but now is the time to build for the future.

60-31 Overall Score or 20-11 Individual Score

This score indicates much organizational deficiency. Small steps of incremental change will not provide enough gains to move successfully into the future. This is a good time for the leaders to reach out for help in implementing creative and innovative success factors described in the organizational model. Ineffectiveness needs to be resolved as quickly as possible. The future will deal harshly with the traditional and inflexible.

30-0 Overall Score or 10-0 Individual Score

This score reflects serious deficiencies. Attention is needed now. Attention is needed for change. This organization may have tremendous potential but it is likely to expire before having a chance to prove it. Major changes are needed quickly.

About the Author

Randall R. Richards is a former president of the Society of Automotive Engineers (SAE International), a 65,000-member international organization. As president of SAE, he advanced a new image for the Society—he was the youngest person to hold the position in 52 years.

He graduated from the University of Missouri-Rolla with a B.S. in Electrical Engineering and is R&D Technology Manager at Caterpillar Inc., based in Peoria, Illinois.

Richards is an international speaker, seminar leader, and leadership facilitator who emphasizes leadership for empowerment. Feedback surveys describe Richards as a personable, high-energy, and talented communicator. In one year, he traveled over 100,000 miles and spoke with more than 14,000 people in 150 cities on four continents.

He believes in, works towards, and always encourages personal and professional growth. He communicates values and vision and builds on a framework of enthusiasm and vitality. He has authored numerous articles in trade, society, and technical periodicals and journals on a range of topics, including excellence in leadership, board governance, global quality, visioning for success, advanced technology, and leadership for empowerment.

Mr. R.R. Richards may be reached at:

Leadership for Empowerment
leadership-empowerment.com
richards@bcscom.com
(309) 249-2562